SQUARE PEGS

A BOOK OF SELF-DISCOVERY FOR WOMEN WITH ADHD

KIM RAINE

authors
AND CO.

DEDICATION

For Mum, Jordan and Amaiyah

xxx

CONTENTS

FOREWORD

In September 2021, I opened my laptop and wrote an email to my publisher, delaying the launch of this book.

I felt gutted. Another goal post moved, another false start.

The truth was I had written the book, well three quarters of it, but it was just *A book*, it wasn't *THE book*, and I knew it. I have learnt that when life is hard and nothing is coming easy, it's usually because something isn't right, especially in business.

I knew what was holding me back, but I was still unsure if I was ready to admit it. Then in December 2021, I finally got myself the ADHD diagnosis that came as no surprise at all but changed everything.

I had been studying ADHD for the previous four years as it had begun to filter into more and more areas of my personal and professional life.

As I read, researched and worked with several diagnosed, undiagnosed, and some totally unaware neurodiverse women, I gained an understanding of what ADHD was and how for many of these women, what little resemblance it had to the *'naughty boy bouncing off the walls'* stereotype it was known for.

I became fascinated by it and 100% sure that not only did I have it, but so did the female line in my family, both up and down.

This is a book for women like my daughter, who is now diagnosed, and who struggled for so long. Another young girl who was completely missed. Also, my mum, who at seventy-four, has navigated undiagnosed without any support or understanding. And, for women like me who somehow managed to hold it together until peri-menopause came along and cracked things right open.

But most of all, this book is for my granddaughter and all subsequent generations who may very well be *Square Pegs.* This is a book to help us help them to be able to be themselves and grow up in a world where they never have to fit in.

In your hands is most definitely *THE book,* dedicated to all *Square Pegs* who have spent their lives trying to be *normal* and keep up and fit in.

This book will permit you never to have to try to be *normal* again. It is for you if you are diagnosed or not, if you think you have ADHD, or if you think someone in your family has ADHD.

I want to tell you the story of my ADHD journey along with the women who I have been able to coach along the way. The names have been changed, and their stories are interwoven, but these are women like you and me.

They are intelligent, successful women who have flown under the ADHD radar simply because they don't fit and possibly never did fit the stereotypical idea, we have of what ADHD is.

ADHD isn't that. In fact, in many, it is quite the opposite, especially in women, where it is often hidden, a well-masked secret that feels like a constant sense of never feeling like you are, do or have enough. Never quite getting it right or feeling like you fit in, which is caused by an internal barrage of fast and exhausting thoughts that leave a jumbled mess.

My dear *Square Pegs*, if you have been looking for your people, we are here and no longer prepared to fit in. It's time to rise!

INTRODUCTION
IT'S HIP TO BE SQUARE

I was shocked when my client told me she had been diagnosed with ADHD. This lady wasn't crazy, far from lazy and was nothing like the hyperactive stereotype I associated ADHD with.

The global head of talent for a massive media company, Jill was the complete opposite of what ADHD was to me.

She was intelligent, focused, charismatic and highly successful. We had worked together for some time, and whilst she had her challenges, she was a fantastic client to work with because she got focused and got results.

ADHD?

No way!

And therein lies one of the biggest problems with ADHD in females and possibly the reason you picked up this book.

ADHD is not what we are led to think.

It is far more complex than being unable to sit still, having twenty tabs open at once or always being late.

It is a condition that affects our brain wiring and nervous systems. It is often misrepresented as negative personality traits such as lazy, unmotivated, disorganised, clumsy, messy, greedy, anxious, depressed, hyper, reckless, impulsive, overemotional, sensitive, fiery...the list goes on.

Living with undiagnosed ADHD leaves us susceptible to these labels that are often placed on us as harshly by ourselves as by others. Labels that fester away undermine our confidence and leave us second-guessing our worth.

Many women who realise later in life that they are the owner of a neurodiverse brain have spent years people-pleasing, comparing, perfecting, striving and drowning in repeated failed attempts to be *normal* and fit in.

Well, you are not *normal* - you are far better than *normal*, and your creative, ingenious, super-fast, tenacious, intelligent brain wasn't made to fit in.

The neurotypical world is full of rules, expectations and guide-lines that don't work for our brains.

This is a book about embracing your neurodiversity and designing a life where you dance to the beat of your own drum so that you find peace with yourself and help pave the way to allow future generations to be themselves, be understood and never have to relentlessly and hopelessly try to squeeze their *Square Peg* brains into society's round holes to please others.

I know from getting my diagnosis that there are days when ADHD feels like a curse. When I am a lost, frustrated, scrambled mess of neurodiversity, and everything seems like hard work.

But then there are other days when you had better buckle up because when my brain is on fire, I am unstoppable.

This is a book that will help you have more of the unstoppable days and more self-compassion, understanding and expectance on the days when your ADHD is running the show.

ADHD is challenging. I am not in the camp that believes it is a superpower. Some days it feels anything but. However, I see the women I work with flying higher than most, even though they don't realise it. Extremely intelligent with lists of qualifications and accomplishments that make them the women we look up to, they have achieved phenomenal success and created extraordinary lives for themselves and their families.

So, are you ready to step up and create the beliefs, systems and strategies that can help you focus on, and maximise the advantages of our high-energy, ingenious, fast-thinking, easy-failing, resilient, solution-focused, kind, empathic, tenacious, creative brain?

This may take some unpicking. There may be much you feel resentful, hurt or angry about that to truly be free, you will need to make peace with and let go, but don't panic, you get to choose when that moment is.

This is your journey. Take your time!

Life is too short to waste it worrying that you aren't enough, or that you are going to let others down, or that you are somehow not good enough, and it's too short to spend half of it looking for your keys!

This is a chance to step up, take control of your destiny and start working with your brain rather than against it.

Not everyone I meet with a late ADHD diagnosis is unhappy with their life. Some are relieved and ready to understand themselves better and create strategies that make their lives easier and more productive.

But for others, it's a different story. Other women have paid an enormous price living with undiagnosed ADHD. They have lost friendships, money, job opportunities, relationships, time and self-esteem. Life has passed them by, leaving them feeling lost, stuck or trapped.

Maybe that's you, and you feel you are in a hopeless situation?

- *A loveless marriage.*
- *An unfulfilling job or business.*
- *Raising children with ADHD, or other challenges.*
- *A rundown house.*
- *An oversized body.*
- *An addictive cycle.*
- *Drowning in debt.*
- *Living in lack.*
- *An overwhelming workload.*
- *Even illness.*

If that's you, and right now you are treading water, maybe even drowning, then know that you have taken the first step by picking up this book and that with the right attitude, i.e., doing some soul-searching work, going a lot easier on yourself and being your own cheerleader, you have every chance of turning things around.

Think back, think how some of your darkest moments have been your greatest conquests.

You are a survivor! You've got this!

The women I work with have spent years in service, to their careers, their children, partners, parents, siblings and family and friends, the list is endless.

They have worn so many hats and roles whilst trying to keep up with society's expectations of how a female should be that they have lost their own identities and no longer know who they are.

One of the biggest things I hear from the women I work with is:

- *I feel lost.*
- *I don't know who I am anymore.*
- *I feel invisible.*
- *I feel out of control.*
- *I'm broken.*
- *I want my smile back.*
- *I'm not good enough.*
- *I am more than this.*

I hear it ALL the time, and if it's how you feel, you are not alone!

I want this book to uplift you and show you the unique talents you have with stories from other women who have discovered later in life that they have ADHD and have learnt to live much calmer, happier lives without giving up their success.

That would only be giving you half the picture though, and I want you to feel seen and to know you're not alone, which means sharing the challenges women with ADHD face every day so that we can see where it shows up in our lives and understand the pressure that we put ourselves under.

Sadly, the number of women realising late in life that they could have ADHD and what that means is growing by the day. The damage those undiagnosed years can do is significant. The constant put-downs by ourselves or others go deeper and deeper as each undiagnosed year passes.

By the time they discover the truth, they have spent a lifetime burying, pushing aside, and stuffing down endless, painful emotions left unresolved, festering under the skin and in the subconscious, like a wound, ready to flare up when they least expect it.

I work with women to clean out those wounds and free some of those emotions. The old hurts, confidence knocks feelings of guilt that bubble away under the surface, manifesting in their bodies and day-to-day lives in the form of the symptoms and behaviours that hold them back from being everything they have the right and the ability to be.

***Caveat... I am not a therapist, and I am not about picking the scabs. I am a coach. I am about cleaning that wound out and moving on.

*ADHD*ers are more sensitive. They have been proven to feel physical and emotional pain more intensely, carrying some of the heaviest emotions such as shame, anger, resentment, guilt and fear longer than others.

This book is about finding the real you under the ADHD and buried pain; as you slowly peel back the layers and start to look at yourself through the lens of ADHD, you will see everything in a different light.

This is your time. This is your chance.

Everything you need for the journey is on these pages; however, there is not just one strategy, no easy pill to pop or formula to follow. ADHD doesn't work like that.

Winning at ADHD means creating your individual framework of habits, tools, strategies and possibly medication if you want to try it and it works for you.

So, buckle up, interact with this book and think of it as a bible.

It's a journey I have been on myself.

Living for forty-seven years with undiagnosed ADHD has been problematic, thrilling, scary and interesting. This has shown up many times with:

- *Burnouts.*
- *Catastrophic and embarrassing emotional explosions.*
- *Dangerous near misses.*
- *Fines and unpaid bills.*
- *Repeated lateness.*
- *Missed flights, (sitting on the floor at airports re-organising my case and loading the kids with stuff to get under the luggage limit was a holiday tradition.)*
- *Forgotten birthdays.*
- *Unfinished courses.*
- *Several Glastonburys.*
- *Missed appointments.*
- *Disordered eating.*
- *Hours spent walking round in circles trying to leave the house.*
- *Binge drinking.*
- *Lost phones, keys and cards.*
- *Numerous false starts.*
- *Broken promises to myself and others.*
- *££££'s wasted.*
- *Time wasted.*
- *Three speed awareness courses attended - from the same speed camera every time!*

- *And years of failures.*

But there have also been some incredible highs, crazy fun times, and many fond memories that I can't help but wonder if they may not have happened were it not for my impulsive, you only live once, get crap done brain!

Organising my wedding with five bridesmaids in under three weeks, one of which I was in Greece for - the registrar was gobsmacked when I booked it.

"You mean this year. But that's less than three weeks away."

"Yeah, I know."

Or packing up a rucksack and heading off around the world for a year on my own at just twenty years old; guess how far ahead I planned that?

You guessed it, about three weeks, just long enough for my visa to come through.

I remember my best friend's brother laughing, saying, *"yeah, right, of course, you are!".*

And yes, of course, I was!

Sending my husband off to Spain to purchase a villa I hadn't seen, then headed out for five years with the kids because I couldn't bear the thought of living a normal life.

I have done so many amazing things that I now know are down to my impulsive, creative, adventurous, live in the moment, not afraid to fail brain.

I always knew I wanted to experience all walks of life, from living on a traveller site to sitting in the Beverly Wiltshire on Rodeo Drive sipping champagne with fellow Entrepreneurs.

I have never wanted my life to be ordinary.

We *ADHD*ers live in, and for the moment, there is no later or tomorrow. There is only now - which has led me to take on too much, over-commit myself and put myself in situations I don't need to be a part of on many occasions.

There have been times when ADHD has pushed me over the edge. Although being diagnosed significantly helped, I have realised that ADHD management is an ongoing labour of love that is best accepted and lent into so you (and those around you) can buckle up and enjoy the ride!

What's in store for you on these pages?

This book is a transformative mixture of neuroscience, coaching, health mentoring, and woo.

First, I would love to tell you more about my story, not because it is special or unusual, but because it is the story of many undiagnosed *Square Pegs*. I want to share with you the moment I fully understood the amazing power of ADHD on a retreat in LA.

Then we will look into ADHD, what it is, and the truth about how and why ADHD presents differently in women; where I know you will have some lightbulb moments and things will start to make more sense.

We will then start untangling you from the stories and beliefs you have after years of undiagnosed ADHD. This will show you where your ADHD has run things in the past and where it is still taking the reins today.

So that you can start to be your true, authentic self, a perfect *Square Peg* with no intention of simply fitting in.

It's about dancing to the beat of your own drum, rather than the one you feel duty-bound to, or others expect of you. You will become self-aware and conscious of who you are and the thoughts, beliefs and values that shape your life.

Did you know we think the same things over and over?

It is believed that around a staggering 95% of the thoughts we have are repetitive.

Just let that sink in for a minute. This means that 95% of what you were thinking about today, you likely thought yesterday and possibly the month and year before that too. This is how we can end up stuck and spend so much of our life on repeat! Making the same mistakes time and again or sitting frozen on the sidelines letting life pass us by because even though it may be bad, it is familiar and comfortable.

What do you spend most of your time thinking about?

Note the thoughts that come into your head most often over the next few days.

How are they affecting your decision-making and how you live your life?

You will learn to trust your strong intuition, listen to your heart and value your judgement that you may have lost confidence in over the years. *Square Pegs* have powerful intuition, better than most, but it is almost too much to put into words sometimes, so it can often be ignored. No more though; you will become an expert in tuning in to your strong internal compass and following the right path.

You will feel instantly when you are out of alignment, or something isn't right, so there will be fewer bad decisions, wasted efforts and time living a life you don't connect with to keep everyone happy.

Then you'll be ready to look at those hurts, the places you fear to go, but this time in a new light, without dragging up years of pain or spending a fortune on therapy.

I am talking about facing headfirst into the truth, making peace, accepting it and letting go.

You will understand why *ADHD*ers feel emotional pain harder and longer than neurotypicals.

Do you find yourself going over and over painful moments from years in the past?

- *The true love who left you.*
- *The friend who let you down.*
- *The mother who belittled you.*

I will show you how to let go because that stuff is weighing you down, and it's time you were liberated.

You will get to know who's running the show, you, ADHD or your ego.

The ego is the part in all of us that wants to be adored and loved, but for neurodivergent women, years of put-downs can make their ego so desperate to be accepted and fit in that it guides the decisions we make, the way we show up in the world and the life we live.

Finally, we will look at the day-to-day things you can do to support your brain. I will introduce you to my three step PEG process, which works with our brains to ensure you only do the stuff that moves you forward in life, rather than chasing shiny objects and making mistakes that keep you stuck.

Square Pegs can be pretty unaware of the pressure we are putting on ourselves; I will show you how you can use stress to your advantage and avoid what I am guessing wouldn't be your first burnout. We'll also be looking at nutrition, exercise, how you can get your brain to buy into prioritising them, and the lifestyle habits you need to start or stop to maximise your potential. These are the natural highs that will fire you up.

Alongside this, I will share simple and effective strategies and solutions that work for my *ADHD*ers.

Most of all, I want you to feel seen and know that you are not alone, so I will use the stories my clients have agreed to share along with my own as we work through.

Whilst there are many advantages to ADHD, this book isn't a fairytale.

Living with ADHD is bloody hard at times. I am not here to sugarcoat it. I am certainly not going to be telling you that you are lucky to have some form of superpower because as a peri-menopausal, later diagnosed mum of two, nanny to one and wife to one hell of a lucky man, there are days when my ADHD feels every bit the invisible disability it is.

This is not a deep dive into what ADHD is. It is a look at how it shows up in your life personally and what you can do about it. Don't just read it. Work through it, and give yourself time and space to percolate feelings, ideas and lightbulb moments. I want this book to be your companion, don't hurry it.

Are you ready for this?

Let's begin!

1

LOSE THE LABEL WEAR THE BADGE

"I do hope Kim overcomes her inability to exercise self-discipline. She has a lovely personality, and it is a pity that this is not always seen. Her academic efforts have continued to be inconsistent, while her conduct has often been disruptive. Seven minor misconduct reports were issued. Is it too late to hope for improvement?"

— MRS T - HEAD OF YEAR MARCH 1988,

"Kim has a lot of natural ability but poor self-discipline and motivation. She's her own worst enemy. She cannot see the necessity to apply herself fully to written work and prefers to chat throughout the lesson. Kim shows evidence of a bright and exploring mind when it suits her. However, Kim's report shows that she is working well below her true capabilities and turning her attention to less constructive activities. Her fourteen blue slips indicate Kim can be distracted and lack attention in the classroom, seriously hampering her process. Does Kim wish to give the present impression into most areas?"

— MR J - HEAD OF YEAR, MARCH 1987

My personal favourite because it is still something I struggle with to this day!

> *"Kim must resist the temptation to fill silences with a wisecrack."*

> — MISS J HISTORY

I was the girl in the class that stuck out. I wasn't your typical little girl; I was more like a boy. I had all this energy and struggled to listen unless I was interested in what you were saying.

If you were slightly boring or unable to engage the class and hold interest, then I would struggle to sit in your class and would end up, I am still ashamed to say, being disruptive.

I remember being in the Head of Year's office (again) one day and him telling me (again) that I should be in a higher band and the top classes, but they couldn't risk me disrupting the others, which I knew to be true on all levels.

Then he asked me, *"Kim, what's wrong at home? We want to help you. What's going on that's causing you to behave like this?"*

"Nothing's wrong at home," I said, *"everything's great, I just get bored and like having a laugh, I try not to be disruptive but just can't help it"* reading that back, it sounds like a rude and disrespectful reply, but it was the truth. I really couldn't help it.

I would get this energy surge through me that I didn't know what to do with, so without a healthy outlet, I usually did something stupid and that stayed with me well into adulthood.

I was loud and untamed at school. Most teachers and pupils knew who I was for all the wrong reasons. I had friends and lots of fun, and although I never got in serious trouble or caused harm to anyone but myself, I was known as a *troublemaker*, the sort of girl your mum didn't want you hanging around with.

In later years, the mention of my school days bought such a rush of shame that I would cross the road to avoid old school friends and shut down any conversation that bought it up. I never showed it as a teen, but I was deeply embarrassed and ashamed of my behaviour because despite having amazing, loving, kind, intelligent parents who taught me good values and manners, I couldn't for the life of me behave myself.

I could not control it, even though I knew and cared about the consequences, I often couldn't stop myself.

Looking back at these reports with my family as part of my research for this book was hilarious. Every single comment screamed ADHD. I don't blame anyone for the fact that my ADHD wasn't diagnosed despite it being so blatantly apparent throughout my school reports.

The research wasn't there in the seventies and eighties when I was at school, and so I was just put down as being a rude, disruptive, *pain in the arse* who preferred to muck about and not pay attention, which in effect was true - school was boring.

I am sure that my teachers would have loved the *"intel"* on what ADHD was and how it affected the children in their classes during their careers!

One of my newly diagnosed clients, an ex-school governor in her sixties, says that schools knew some girls didn't engage, the daydreamers that never did homework, who were always forgetting their equipment and underachieving in class. Now she sees that many of those girls would have had ADHD, which makes her feel sad.

Like me, I am sure they were encouraged to try harder, but that's impossible for an ADHD brain that isn't interested in what's being taught. I know it had the opposite effect on me. Some ADHDers will not be told what to do and are likely to do the complete opposite. Others will try their utmost to please you, even if it means putting themselves through hell. I was and still can be the former. If it doesn't interest me, then sitting quietly can be physical and mental agony for me.

I realised that I undoubtedly had ADHD after spending five hours straight sitting in a room on just a chair, two meters apart due to covid restrictions, without a coffee break listening to something I wasn't interested in. That day was hard I went to the loo about ten times because I couldn't sit still, and I didn't even have a table to hide behind, just me on a plastic chair trying to behave. It was exhausting managing all the excess energy.

I had also been twenty minutes late after having given myself plenty of time to get to the venue, and I was ready on time, but then somehow took twenty minutes to get out of the house. This was an important day that I had invested in being at.

Leaving the house is something I have always struggled with!

At home, I was loved and accepted. It was a happy and safe place, although my mum may be surprised to hear that because I was difficult at home too.

I didn't do any sports or exercise. I loved netball, but I didn't have the drive to go to the practices. I was an overweight teen who was drinking and smoking, as were many of my friends, to be fair.

My life was based around my friends, and like most teenage girls, I was desperate to fit in. Nothing was more important to me, but I was too emotional, too sensitive and easily hurt, and I went through a period of real depression where I struggled to fit in.

I was a size eighteen by the time I was eighteen. My boyfriend was in a band, and every weekend was travelling around the country drinking, smoking and eating late-night kebabs.

I hated exercise. I would drive to a Moves Fitness class at the local school hall, have a cigarette on the way, and spend half the class in the toilet as I needed a breather. Come out, pop in the pub and pick up a curry on the way home.

That side of things changed in my early thirties when I discovered weightlifting—until then, working out had been something I did to manage my weight, which was under better control in my twenties. I was never bothered about being the fittest or the fastest, but the strongest was always something really, really important to me. Strength training changed my life, and I love it.

I split up with my boyfriend just before my twentieth birthday. He was lovely, but my feet were itching, and I just couldn't stay!

Four weeks later, I bought myself a plane ticket and went around the world on my own.

This is in the day before mobile phones, before email, before being able to load up pictures on Instagram to stay in touch with your friends.

I got on that plane and was off around the world completely alone. Looking back, I realise that my spontaneous ADHD brain needed adventure and change. It was one of the best years of my life!

I love looking back at the moments when my brain has taken me off on an adventure, and it's been fantastic. I encourage you to do the same! Think of the times your unique brain has taken you on some adventure others would hesitate at.

Having my daughter at twenty-six changed my life.

I was ill-equipped to become a mum. My partner and I, now my husband, had been together and had been the best of *friends with benefits* for many years, but only officially as a couple for six weeks... and I was six weeks pregnant for the first time in my life!

My pregnancy was totally unplanned, which I am sure doesn't surprise you. It didn't surprise me. I never planned anything. Having a baby didn't make sense, but there was something inside of me telling me this was the right thing to do despite all the evidence. I felt instantly connected, and all sense and reason went out the window.

She was the most amazing thing that's ever happened to me, I was instantly in love, but motherhood was a million times harder than I'd ever imagined. The overwhelm of being responsible for another human being was a shock and growing into a responsible parent over night, just wasn't going to happen!

We moved to Spain, eighteen months after my son was born, just after my thirtieth birthday.

Many of my friends still didn't have children, and I knew being around them was just too much of a distraction from family life plus, we were both ready for an adventure by then, so we sold up and moved to Javea in Spain. These were very happy times, and I had the head space to concentrate on my family.

I had always had so many people in my life. We were both still young and lived in the village we grew up in. We loved the pub and had lots of friends, which was great, but my ADHD brain, who views everything as equally important, struggled to differentiate between who and what mattered and how much.

I would find myself embroiled in other people's lives, always trying to help or being the shoulder to cry on, giving time away that I didn't have that I should have been spending with my family and kids. Moving away stripped all of that back. Life was so simple…ish!

My ADDCA (ADD Coaching Academy) tutor, Barbara Luther, talked about people with ADHD having this uncomfortable feeling in their bodies. For me, this showed up as always wanting to be somewhere else, always wanting to be moving on or working on the next idea. Even if we were standing watching the children play, I could never fully be in the moment for long.

I was torn and guilt-ridden trying to balance motherhood and work. Although that isn't exclusive to ADHD, I think most working mothers would be able to relate to that one. I didn't seem to be able to switch off, though, wherever I was, my brain was always buzzing, planning and creating. My mind was racing with ideas, problems, and solutions… negative, positive it was always on the go.

I found parenting a challenge. That is where I regret not knowing I had ADHD the most. My children are my greatest achievement, and I am so proud of them. They are great level-headed, happy humans, and I love watching them grow every minute. However, raising them with undiagnosed ADHD was a white-knuckle ride for all of us at times, *thank goodness for my laid-back husband.*

Things ramped up in my early forties when I struggled with my energy and my sleep, experiencing anxiety for the first time.

I couldn't focus, was impulsive, couldn't see anything through, my brain bounced all over the place, and I struggled with frequent burnouts.

Then, in 2019, just after selling my business, I discovered I was going to be a grandparent at the age of forty-six, at least five years ahead of time, and my ADHD took on a life of its own.

I am not sure any mother would rejoice at their twenty-year daughter and her partner telling you she is pregnant and having a baby. I was scared on so many levels.

The birth didn't go according to plan, ending in a C Section that left my daughter life-threateningly ill for forty-eight hours shortly afterwards. But there was no time to process it because coronavirus started to ramp up, and a month later, we were all in lockdown.

When they needed support, they were stuck in a flat and isolated from everyone. My ADHD symptoms seemed to hit a new level.

I became impulsive and went into hyper-focus, putting everyone on edge in my efforts to make everything alright and do everything I could. I know I wasn't the only *ADHD*er who felt like this at the time. We are amazing in a crisis, galvanising everyone and making things happen, but we need to be careful that we don't become overbearing in our actions or opinions.

Whilst all this was happening, I was becoming aware of the perimenopause kicking in, my body was changing, and things had shifted. Rather than three decent weeks and one bad one, it slowly become several tougher weeks and a few good days. I felt completely out of control. My brain was foggy, and I couldn't concentrate on anything for long, I was bouncing all over the show, struggling to make simple decisions.

I had seen the relief and clarity a diagnosis gave clients, and I knew it was time, but there was still a part of me who was quietly worried about the *label* and what people would think.

"I'm not surprised. She always was all over the show" you know the sort of things you can conjure up when you let your imagination run wild.

I got my diagnosis in December 2021, four years since I'd first started looking into ADHD, thanks to Jill's diagnosis.

I cried for what ADHD had cost me, rather than others, for the first time when the Psychiatrist's report came through the letter box. There laid out in front of me were all the times things had been hard, and I had assumed it was because I was weak, bad, stupid or not enough. Too emotional, over-sensitive, lazy, greedy, the list goes on.

I didn't cry for long; I just tucked it away and kept it to myself for a while, sharing it with only my close friends, family and clients. People I knew I wouldn't have to defend myself against and answer relentless questions about why I think I have ADHD. I wasn't in the headspace to fight the many opinions people have on ADHD.

Because despite seeing the changes in the women before me, I was still not ready to have the label of ADHD.

That all changed on a beach in LA one March.

I was with my coach Lisa Johnson and the rest of her Destination Inspiration *Masterminders*. It was the end of a phenomenal few days, and we were rounding it off with some hot seat/brainstorming sessions on the beach.

I asked what I should be doing.

I had been coaching women for sixteen years. I knew about menopause, mindset, sleep, burnout, nutrition, exercise, weight loss, hormones, neuroscience, and mindfulness, and I loved it all, but I didn't know where it was all directing me, and I felt a bit lost.

The group were amazing. There is nothing like sitting in a powerful circle with your peers. You get the truth.

Eventually, someone said, *"What do you actually want to do, Kim, because you are bouncing around all over the show?"*

I laughed and said, *"I know. It's the bloody ADHD."*

"That's it. That is what you need to do," she said. We had already spoken about it, but I was holding back. Then everyone in the group began to agree, saying I came alive when I talked about it, which had been a lot. I was hyper focused on my learning. I wanted to know everything, and like many of my fellow *Square Pegs*, I'm a verbal processor, so I like to talk!

As they began telling me how much it was needed and why I was the lady to do it, I felt sick to my stomach.

I told them I didn't feel ready to tell the world I have ADHD. Then I asked a question that changed it all.

"How many of you have or think you have ADHD?"

Out of about thirty people, seven or eight put their hand up, and several others hovered as they either weren't sure or, like me, weren't ready to admit it, and there were a few who at that point had no idea they had ADHD, but by that time I was pretty good at spotting it.

It hit me; these weren't thirty ordinary people. These were thirty phenomenal Entrepreneurs who had stepped out of the norm and were sitting *working* on a beach in LA, running highly profitable, successful businesses. Wow.

They weren't there in spite of their ADHD; they were more likely there because of it.

Their insatiable drive, ingenious, creative, super-fast brains and the tenacity to always keep going had got them there, and I was so proud to be there with them.

It suddenly struck me that everything amazing about ADHD was sat in this circle.

At that moment, my whole perspective changed.

I thought of the emails and DMs I'd received from people who suspected ADHD could be the issue but were afraid of being given a *label*. Parents were saying, *"I think my child's got ADHD, but I don't want them to have the label"*, or from women who were afraid to tell clients and people at work because they felt embarrassed or judged.

I thought about my granddaughter and all the future generations who would be held back from understanding their brains and how to get the best out of them if we are afraid of the judgement a diagnosis might bring.

It wasn't about hiding from the label, it was about wearing the badge and celebrating all of the phenomenal potentials that were available if you just knew how to work with your brain rather than trying to make it work like everyone else's.

There are so many hidden gems in our neurodiverse brains, and whilst ADHD makes life harder and more challenging in some instances, so does being born into poverty, a physical disability, or a traumatic start in life.

Life is hard for many people for many reasons, but a shift in perspective can make all the difference, and I left LA ready to *Lose the Label and Wear the Badge* and celebrate the amazing advantages of ADHD.

When my husband picked me up from the airport a few days later, I was buzzing.

I told him of my plans and what I was going to do, and then I said, *"The best thing is I can be myself now"* I felt the emotion trapped like a lump in my throat, it took my breath away, and I realised how much of myself I'd hidden away, especially within my business.

I've always known I could do better, but I was the queen of distraction and self-sabotage and assumed, just like at school, it was because I wasn't trying hard enough. I now know I was trying harder than most. Yet, rather than moving forward, I was like a squash ball on a court bouncing from one wall to the next.

Leaning into my ADHD has changed so many aspects of my life. I never try to hide it, and I never use it as an excuse, but it is an explanation, there are things that my brain cannot do, but there is plenty that it can. I cut myself slack and no longer try to work harder when something isn't working. Instead, I pause and ask myself how MY brain needs to do this.

I'm excited for the future of women with ADHD, I think we have some groundbreaking years ahead of us, but we all have to play our part in leading the way and championing our brain. I'm not going to hide behind my ADHD anymore, maybe you don't feel the same or have people you cannot tell, and that's ok. The right time will come.

2

YOUR BEAUTIFUL BRAIN

"ADHD makes life paradoxical.

You can super focus, but you can also space out when you least mean to. You can radiate confidence and also feel as insecure as a cat in a kennel. You can perform at the highest level, feeling incompetent as you do so. You can be loved by so many, but feel as if no one really likes you. You can absolutely totally intend to do something, then forget to do it. You can have the greatest ideas in the world, but feel as though you can't accomplish a thing"

— DR EDWARD M HALLOWELL

I described my brain to my husband as a big scribble, there is lots of information in there, but it is impossible to unscramble and pick the important stuff out at times.

Here is how my clients & members of my ADHD *Brains In Business* community, most of who have been diagnosed *(self or otherwise)* in their late adulthood, described their brains:

- *A beautiful mess.*
- *Like a dog in a field of squirrels, always trying to multi-task but never getting far, very easily distracted, highly emotional and pretty scrambled.*
- *Fuzzy, like having TV static in my head.*
- *I've never considered it noisy, but I think the static is my brain trying to quieten my inner voice.*
- *All over the place!*
- *Impulsive with some things, over-thinker on others.*
- *Decision paralysis is real.*
- *Like a popcorn machine that overheats and then goes into a cool-down mode when you need it the most!*
- *Multidirectional.*
- *Exceptional, creative, ambitious, and easily overwhelmed by the mundane.*
- *0-70 in 1.2 seconds or stalling every five seconds!!*
- *Super, fiery and running at a million miles an hour.*
- *A chaotic jumble.*

What is ADHD?

Attention Deficit Hyperactivity Disorder is not a behaviour or discipline problem; it is a brain disorder caused by genetic, neurological and environmental factors that affect the production or uptake of the brain's chemical messengers (neurotransmitters) Dopamine, Serotonin and Noradrenaline. These messengers play a significant role in memory, reward, motivation and the ability to maintain attention.

With ADHD, these messages can be slow, lost or scrambled, especially in the limbic system, Amygdala, cerebellum and prefrontal cortex that governs Executive Functioning.

Executive Function refers to the brain circuits that prioritise, integrate and control self-regulation. Dr Thomas Brown PhD's lists these functions as Activation, Focus, Effort, Emotion, Memory and Action.

He describes it as the brain's management system that helps us to:

- Act and respond appropriately.
- Practise self-restraint or inhibition.
- Transition and shift between activities or tasks.
- Organise, prioritise and activate.
- Focus and sustain attention.
- Regulate and control emotion.
- Make a plan and stick to it.
- Monitor and access our behaviour.
- Utilise working memory and access recall so that we can predict possible outcomes and learn from past experiences.

Here are a few facts

Although not used in ADHD diagnosis, recent studies with fMRI imaging show areas of the brain that control many ADHD symptoms to be about 3-5% smaller.

There is a 30% delay in the development of the ADHD brain that affects the thickening of the brain's cortical areas that control executive functioning, social behaviours and maturity. It is important to note that this does not affect our intelligence or IQ.

Square Pegs are smart but stuck!

According to Dr Russell Berkley, this delay means an eighteen-year-old with ADHD is more like a twelve-year-old in mental maturity. This gap between chronological and developmental age can cause big issues with behaviours, friendships, motivation, interests, emotional regulation, decision making, drive and vulnerability at a critically important time in a child's impressionable life. Causing frustration and misunderstanding between these teens, their carers and sometimes teachers, adding to negative feelings and lack of confidence.

It's not yet known if this delay is lessened, but many researchers believe it is one of the reasons that *Square Pegs* are younger at heart than their peers.

We know that ADHD is not caused by bad parenting, teaching, social economics or too much sugar, although all that can be damaging to already existing ADHD.

Sidenote Many professionals believe this delay to be nearer to 6-10 years in children, with the gap closing as we age. Something to bear in mind if you're raising Square Pegs now, especially if you feel like you are failing, being judged or being criticised for your parenting skills.

It's a family affair

If you have ADHD, there is a high chance someone in your close family does too. It's highly genetic, with one study finding mothers of ADHD children twenty-four times more likely than the average woman to have ADHD themselves and fathers five times.

Just because you have ADHD in your family line doesn't mean you will all have the same traits and symptoms. It can look very different from person to person, even within the same family.

The line will likely go up a generation as well as down. If you are suffering from trauma or issues from your childhood thanks to your upbringing, then it is worth bearing in mind that there will have been many men and women before us who never had the information we are lucky to have now. And therefore, the chance to help and understand the diagnosis would have been rare.

ADHD Types

If you have a diagnosis, you will likely have been placed into one of the following three categories that medical professionals use to help understand the predominant traits, challenges and behaviours of ADHD.

Predominately Hyperactive and Impulsive ADHD - excessive talking, constant moving, high energy, interruptive, low self-control, fidgeting and tapping. This type is more common in children and men.

Predominately Inattentive ADHD (Formally known as ADD) - easily distracted, daydreams, loses things, makes careless mistakes, misses deadlines, low motivation, struggles to listen, appears uninterested, this type is more common in females.

Inattentive types tend to live in their heads and struggle more with executive functioning. They hide and mask their ADHD well so it can be missed until later in life when the demands of school, higher education or "adulting" ramp up.

Combined Type Combined types have six symptoms of both and are the most common.

In his book, Dr Daniel Amen, a psychiatrist and brain imaging specialist, claims there are seven types of ADHD, each with its own symptoms and needing its own treatment. This research is in its infancy right now but is very promising. His TEDx Talk is well worth a watch.

Common Symptoms

Some ADHD symptoms can seem like personality traits, causing many women, including myself, to assume that everyone feels like this, and it must just be them. Everyone does feel the symptoms below at times. However, in the case of ADHD, they have been present and causing significant challenges and difficulties since childhood.

Which ones resonate with you, and when do you first recall noticing them?

- Overly emotional
- Daydreaming
- Driven
- Easily distracted
- Forgetful
- Struggle with high and low energy
- Highly Sensitive
- Hyperfocused
- Overly Talkative - blurts out and interrupts
- Can appear careless or scatty
- Creative
- Frequent burnouts
- Addictive
- Trouble listening
- Unmotivated
- Resourceful
- Poor time-keeping
- Overspending
- Indecision
- Trouble meeting deadlines

- Low self-esteem
- High Achieving
- Avoiding tedious, boring tasks but hyper-focusing on others
- Struggles to complete tasks
- Physically, mentally and verbally impulsive.

This is how my community described their ADHD on a day-to-day basis.

- *'A constant fight to focus on things that I need to do.'*
- *'Inability to focus and prioritise. If I don't have a written list, nothing will get done.'*
- *'I'm easily distracted, inefficient and live in a permanent state of overwhelm. I fidget constantly, and I'm bad for interrupting people while they're talking. I have very low self-esteem and self-worth, but if you ask others, they'd say I'm very confident. I'm a perfectionist, but it's detrimental as nothing is ever good enough, so it never gets completed. Constantly feeling like I'm not good enough or less than.'*
- *'Endless procrastination and underachieving.'*
- *'Rarely finishing a task, feeling apathetic, unproductive, disordered eating, self-critical, procrastinating, overwhelmed, forgetting things. On the plus side, if I'm doing something I enjoy, particularly something that uses my hands (perhaps more than my brain), I can focus and get stuff done.'*
- *'Anxious, muddled, and organised whilst swimming against a deluge of doubt and indecision, my senses are overloaded.'*
- *'Overwhelming and exhausting.'*
- *'A mixture of very focused activities until distracted or extremely difficult to start the day regardless of how much planning I've put in place the night before.'*

- *'A regular feeling of achieving very little each day, even though I know I've done loads.'*
- *'Feeling stupid due to, at times being unable to finish the simplest of tasks.'*
- *'Complete euphoria when thinking of a new project/business idea/ shiny gadget, where whatever I'm working on is completely obliterated from my brain.'*
- *'Regularly trying to stay on track and reel myself back from new ideas, distractions and shiny objects.'*
- *'Spinning too many plates, alertness, fear of forgetting something, a restlessness of not completing things. Easily distracted, but I enjoy those journeys at times too.'*
- *'Intense, exhausting, constantly thinking.'*

How come everyone suddenly had ADHD?

Due to the vast and varied symptoms, ADHD isn't easy to diagnose, meaning it is often misdiagnosed and is still seriously underdiagnosed, especially in older women.

Doctors believe that between 75-85% of those who could have ADHD are still not diagnosed.

Research, understanding and developments in neuroscience move fast, and week by week, we are discovering more about how our brains work.

ADHD wasn't believed to affect girls when I was young, it was something hyperactive adolescent boys had, and therefore all the research was done on, you guessed it, prepubescent boys. Meaning inattentive types and girls like me were overlooked, written off and labelled talkative, dreamy or disruptive.

Inattentive and Adult ADHD wasn't diagnosed until the 1990s.

This meant that, like me, many women of my generation never had the help and support to succeed that our male peers did. Even now, boys are four times more likely to be diagnosed than girls as the presentation of symptoms can be so much more disruptive and obvious.

Thanks to new research, increased awareness and social media, there is a rise in older women (and some men too) who have spent their lives masking symptoms—feeling they are somehow less than or not enough, finally getting a diagnosis and the chance to understand how their brains work differently.

*ADHD*ers aren't better, worse, more or less intelligent. We are different, that's all! and I am incredibly grateful that at the grand old age of forty-eight, I finally got the chance to understand how my brain works

Everyone doesn't *suddenly* have ADHD. We always have; we are just *suddenly* getting diagnosed.

Side NoteWhilst the overall feeling is relief and validation, many women still go through a period where they reflect on the loss they have suffered and feel grief around where they knew things could have been different.*

One of my clients in her early sixties, just a year away from retirement, has recently been diagnosed after years of working with psychiatrists and therapists for General Anxiety Disorder - GAD. One day in a session, I brought up the subject of ADHD. She was surprised, saying surely that would have been picked up by now. She had spent years on medication and working with professionals to stabilise her mental health.

A week later, she returned and told me her psychiatrist had referred her for an ADHD assessment. Six weeks later, she had a diagnosis. Several months later, and still trying to stabilise her symptoms, she said there were times she wishes she didn't know because she feels it's too much to deal with and too late. Still, she also knows she has years ahead of her and finding the right medication and learning new strategies make those happier and peaceful.

When you get a diagnosis, there is a lot to reflect on and come to terms with, and the awareness as you understand better and reflect on past events can be equally enlightening and over-whelming at times. I believe a diagnosis is always the right answer, you may feel differently, and that's ok too. The choice is yours.

ADHD rarely travels alone

50% of people with ADHD are known to suffer from a co-existing condition. These are often diagnosed before ADHD or diagnosed instead of ADHD and include learning difficulties, emotional difficulties and physical illness too.

Some of the conditions commonly found with ADHD are:

- Alcoholism and addiction
- Eating disorders
- Autism
- Dyslexia
- Dyscalculia
- Motor and Oral Tics, including Tourette's syndrome
- Premenstrual dysphoric disorder (PMDD)
- Bipolar
- Depression
- Obesity

- Insomnia
- Anxiety
- Bad behaviour/poor parenting
- Generalised Anxiety Disorder
- PMS
- Restless leg syndrome
- Fibromyalgia and other autoimmune conditions
- ME/Chronic Fatigue Syndrome

But I'm not hyperactive

The excessive energy present in all *ADHD*ers isn't always physical. *Square Pegs* may not be visibly hyperactive; you may feel the opposite, where just climbing upstairs feels like a mountain, but hyperactivity can be cognitive, like mental restlessness in the mind and body.

Cognitive hyperactivity can present as:

- Racing thoughts
- Excessive talking
- Constant ideas
- Fast-talking
- Interrupting
- Easily bored
- Multi-tasking
- Insomnia
- Overworking
- Difficulties listening (someone mentions a person in conversation, and your brain wanders off thinking of that person. Two minutes later, you have no ideas what the person talking to has been saying.)

Cognitive hyperactivity shows up as a need to always be moving forward, on to the next thing and the next, never stopping to celebrate or acknowledge achievements.

This mental restlessness makes being in the moment physically uncomfortable and leads to the constant feeling of never being, having or doing enough I see in most *Square Pegs*. It can feel relentless and one of the reasons for the high levels of anxiety many struggle with.

The comedian and influencer Russell Brand is an excellent example of cognitive hyperactivity; he is a fast talker and thinker. Interestingly, he has overcome his pretty extreme additions by learning to pause and control his mind using meditation, mindfulness and therapy.

Pausing is the P in the PEG process that is vital for managing cognitive hyperactivity and most ADHD symptoms. I will introduce you to it later because learning to pause is a game changer for managing ADHD.

Fidgeting for focus

Physical restlessness is another outlet for the excess energy that has nowhere to go, especially when bored or tired.

Physical hyperactivity can look like:

- Fidgeting
- Need to get up and move
- Rocking
- Twisting hair
- Playing with jewellery, pens or toys
- Tapping

- Leg jiggling
- Doodling
- Shifting position
- Chewing
- Teeth grinding
- Playing with your hands,

Not all hyperactivity is bouncing up and down. Although I have known some high-energy *Square Pegs* who do this subtlety in conversation, it is just a part of their personality.

Movement and fidgeting have been shown to improve focus and memory. Even chewing can help concentration, so don't try and stop it because you need to do it!

There are lots of fidget items available. I have seen beautiful rings that you can subtly play with during conversations and meetings, as well as pens and toys. Using props can also help; I struggle to listen if I haven't got a pen in my hand.

How do we operate?

Square Peg brains are wired for interest. We don't do boring or mundane very well. In fact, we don't do it if we can help it, no matter how important the task is to ourselves or those we love. It's not that we *won't* but more often that we *can't*; our brain literally says *No!*

Find something we are interested in, and it slips into hyper focus, becoming so intensely consumed we lose all interest or awareness of other tasks, situations or commitments around us, leaving everything else behind in its wake, including the important stuff.

This is called situational variability and is the cause of the invisible and frustrating ADHD paradox that leads to so much misunderstanding and school reports like mine in the previous chapter. Our ability depends on the environment and interests.

Hyper focus is one of the ADHD traits often referred to as a superpower. When focused in the right direction and coupled with our high energy, creative mind and insatiable drive, it is just that. Untamed, it can be a destructive burden that can lead to bad habits, addiction, wasted hours, and be overbearing for those around us who don't share our excitement, interest or urgency.

A few things need to be in place to harness hyper focus's positive side.

Interest, urgency and a clear outcome.

If the goal is exciting and interesting, we are in, like IN!

All the way, I bet people have watched you in awe as you have steamed through a project or task that you are passionate about.

When it is mundane and uninteresting, no matter how important or who is relying on us, we struggle to get the task done. This leaves us with incomplete projects and half-done ideas as we struggle to tie up the boring loose ends or run out of interest before we get to the finish line.

Whilst the neurotypical brain can prioritise tasks due to their importance, we only see a task as important if it is interesting. Our lack of urgency over something the outside world sees as important can be infuriating for those around us, often leaving them baffled as they will have seen us executing large tasks with impressive efficiency and effectiveness. Yet, we can't pay our car tax or get to the meeting on time.

ADHD is essentially about interest, anticipation and novelty. Importance, threats, rewards or consequences are not good motivators for us and will cause us to withdraw, but make it interesting and exciting, and we are in.

We live in the present moment, which is approximately four seconds long; there is either now or not. Struggling to connect to our future selves, we easily discount our future needs making achieving long-term goals challenging for us. Even when we are aware of the consequences or committed to the future, we struggle to resist immediate pressures or temptations.

Experts call this *Temporal Discounting* - the inability to make decisions or sacrifices that affect the future in the present moment. Walter Mischel's famous marshmallow test, where he offered a small child the chance to get two marshmallows instead of the one on offer if they could wait fifteen minutes for it, is the perfect example of *Temporal Discounting*. It's about taking the small rewards now rather than waiting for the big reward later.

In the adult world, this looks like this:

- *The glass of wine right now feels much more important than losing weight for a future event.*
- *Saving for your retirements versus going on holiday.*
- *Ditching the report writing to go to the pub.*
- *Sticking it on the credit card to pay later.*

Square Pegs aren't patient; we have a stronger aversion to waiting than others, and if the goal is too far away, we will struggle to stay excited and motivated enough to see it through to the end.

Having structures in place that support our goals is vital. Working with the right coaches and experts in achieving that goal and understanding how our brains work can be a good investment but take your time and trust your instinct when building a support team.

Try using vision boards and visual reminders to bring your goals to life, move them around and make updates to keep them at the top of your mind; we stop seeing the things in front of us after a while if they stay the same.

Knowing the end goal and working backwards with regular mini goals to achieve and celebrate is key to keeping interest. Remember, we get bored easily, no interest, no action! It has to stay interesting and exciting.

Side Note *Square Pegs can end up in debt easily; spending and eating are the top impulsive traits of women, both places we see temporal discounting. If this is you, then don't be ashamed. It is not you; it is the way your brain works. Speak to a debt agency that can help you consolidate your debts and get back on track. Then put a freeze on or get rid of credit cards. Try using the more modern banks that allow savings in one account - some you can even tie up longer term. I find these banks far more ADHD friendly. Something that has worked for me is celebrating not buying something by putting the money I don't spend into my Money Not Spent pot. I put everything from a coffee to an item of clothing in, and I get a real buzz watching it grow (I still get that all-important dopamine hit that spending can give us, but I get to keep the money! #win)*

Time after time

We struggle with time. Vastly overestimating the time tasks we find boring take, underestimating the quick five-minute tasks we think we can fit in and losing time in the tasks we love and find interesting. We don't feel it passing, easily over-scheduling ourselves leaving us feeling exhausted and overwhelmed, having to reluctantly or embarrassingly cancel events.

We often miss the urgency of running out of time until we have run out of time or driven everyone waiting for us crazy.

You know the sort of thing:

- *My appointment is in five minutes.*
- *But I live six minutes away.*
- *If the traffic is good.*
- *It will be fine, as long as there is a space in front of the building.*
- *And they are running a few minutes late themselves.*
- *I haven't even got my shoes on yet and need a wee before I go.*
- *Oh crap, I am late!*
- *How the hell did that happen?*

Time blindness is one of the reasons so many of us ram our schedules, overestimating what we can achieve and underestimating the time it will take us.

How often do you feel stressed or running late because you have tried to fit a ten-minute job into a five-minute window?

Welcome to my life!

I had a friend who was always a few minutes early, and time-keeping was important to him. Sadly, I was always a few minutes late.

He even got me a place on a time-keeping course his company ran. I proudly posted the certificate online, and this was it. I would never be late again.

Until the next time we met, I was five minutes late, and he couldn't hide his annoyance. To him, I completely disregarded his time and our friendship, but nothing could have been further from the truth; his friendship meant everything to me, and I had the utmost respect for him and his time.

I really had no idea why I was always late either. It was another one of those *Square Peg* what the hell is wrong with me moments!

Side note Not all Square Pegs are late, in fact, some struggle with time in a different way, they are always early, and the fear that they will be late can consume them for hours before an appointment to the detriment of all else. It is another form of hyper-focus.

Putting it off

Square Pegs are master procrastinators, relying on the urgency a looming deadline brings to release the cortisol and adrenaline that fires up in our brains and helps us focus and kicks us into action.

The struggle to get started and going was one of my biggest challenges. Difficulty transitioning between tasks meant I often wasted a whole day procrastinating and putting off an important task, taking it right to the deadline and finishing in a flurry of cortisol and adrenaline.

Procrastination is about not wanting to do the thing for one reason or another, so we find something else to do instead, as we don't want to feel uncomfortable. Instantly reducing our chances of taking any action on the other thing.

Perfectionism is another common form of procrastination for *Square Pegs*, which we will discuss in the following chapters.

Long lists of to-dos can cause procrastination. Where the list can feel so overwhelming or boring that we pick the quick and easy bits and bobs, so we feel like we are achieving something, but we are just doing the minimal tasks that don't move us forward.

Side note Hands up if you have ever put completed tasks on your to-do list so you can tick them off? Yep, me too!

What sort of a procrastinator are you?

- *The Thrill Seeker* - you like to experience the adrenaline or love the *rush* of beating the clock...just!
- *The Ostrich* - you fear failure (or success), so you delay tasks to protect yourself.
- *The Ditherer* - you end up frozen because you can't make the decision.
- *The Perfectionist* - forever tweaking, researching, adjusting and delaying because it is not right?
- *The Busybee* - doing quick and easy tasks that give you a buzz of completing a task but not the one you're putting off.

For *Square Pegs* to avoid procrastinating, you need a clear plan. The environment needs to be right; with everything you need to hand, distractions out of sight, especially your phone, and your brain needs to be ignited. Which for me usually means listening to some music.

Despite loving a workout, I still struggle to get to the gym most mornings. I would find all manner of things to do and then spend half the time on my phone once I was in there.

I know that the part where I need the most energy and focus is getting to the gym, so I have a starting time to aim for that I give myself a thumbs up every time I make it on time. I then immediately write down my plan, pump out some tunes, put my phone out of sight and use a timer and intervals throughout my workout to keep me on track, and it works like a dream most days!

Tune In

What are your takeaways from this chapter?

What parts resonated with you the most?

How can you use what you have just learned to help you manage your day-to-day symptoms better?

3

ADHD IN FEMALES

Historically the belief was that ADHD was outgrown by adulthood and rarely found in girls. We now know this isn't the case. However, there is still a huge gender gap in ADHD diagnosis, with boys four times more likely to be diagnosed early than girls.

Women have been excluded from scientific and medical research for centuries, with many illnesses or changes put down to hysteria, including menopause, epilepsy and ADHD symptoms.

I have lost count of clients over the years who have come to me on anti-depressants after many visits to the GP for symptoms they struggle to explain. When the GPs cannot diagnose, they are offered a tablet and leave feeling like they can't cope. Thinking it is down to them and that they need to try harder.

ADHD in women is far more of an inside job, often a well-kept secret, with hyperactivity being more cognitive than physical, causing fast thinking and overwhelming thoughts that can result in a negative internal dialogue and shame forcing them further into themselves.

Women are more commonly diagnosed with ADHD inattentive type (previously known as ADD, Attention Deficit Disorder), the quieter, more hidden ADHD. They are better at hiding their less obvious symptoms masking their true feelings and mimicking the behaviour of their neurotypical peers to fit in and appear *normal.*

These women are often exhausted, physically and mentally, leaving them overwhelmed as to where to start. Years of relentlessly pushing forward and continuing at all costs can take their toll.

So much is expected of us, and never have we felt so under pressure. Women are told we can *have it all,* but this is not matched with equal workloads in the home or societal expectations.

The truth is it never will be. It cannot possibly be. Evolution simply won't allow it.

Our hormones, our brains, culture and upbringing all shape the women we become. To look at how ADHD presents so differently in females, let's look at the fundamental differences in females' physiology.

Females are made to care; we are programmed to people please, it is in our physiology, and it starts the minute we are born!

In her amazing book *'The Female Brain',* Louann-Brizendine MD tells us how all brains begin life as female until those that will be male get a surge of testosterone at eight weeks in utero, creating more cells in the sex and aggression centres. Whilst the female fetal brain will begin to sprout more connections in the communication and emotion centres, making her more talkative and caring than a male.

The first thing a female brain does is study faces; I see this so much in my granddaughter. I watch the concentration on her face as she looks deep into my eyes and responds to my emotional signals. Whilst boys do look at faces; they will look more at the environment first. In fact, a baby girl's eye contact and facial gazing skills will increase 400% in their first three months, whereas boys will not increase at all. This is because that testosterone surge in utero also shrinks a male's centre for communication, observation and emotional processing.

Girls love faces; they are reading emotional expressions all the time and learn how to interact with others. They can tell if they are loved, irritating, worthy, or annoying. This is why women are so good at knowing what people are thinking, and it is why we must trust our intuition. We know!

Expression is vital to girls. Having a mother who's depressed, unresponsive or had too much botox can make them feel rejected, but they learn quickly they can get the reaction they want by doing the right thing. They are learning how to people please and be socially accepted.

This is why girls mature and develop one to two years faster than boys.

Women can even hear a broader range of tones in voices than males. It's how we can pick up on even the slightest agitation in a voice, whereas men generally can't. The trouble is we assume they can, which is why when you feel annoyed, hurt, or rejected, most men have no clue unless you tell them exactly how you are feeling. Which is a much better solution than leaving things to fester for days, putting out clues for them to catch on to, except they can't. Male brains aren't wired to pick up the unspoken unless it is danger, then they react.

Anthropologists think that this is why women generally cry much easier than men so that men can get the message!

We are wired for empathy; female babies just twenty-four hours old respond to the cries of other babies, and little girls as young as one will respond to the distress of others. I see this with my granddaughter too; I was blown away the first time I pretended to cry. She immediately jumped on my lap, held my face and gave me what was a very sloppy but beautiful kiss.

Baby girls are so observant and able to pick up on emotions that they easily incorporate the mother's nervous system into their own. Epigenetic imprinting, which is less strong in boys, means that a mother's emotional state in the first two years can be absorbed at a cellular and neurological level changing the girl's perception of reality, affecting their outlook for the rest of their life.

Fantastic if you have a calm, happy mother, not so great if you have a mother with undiagnosed or unsupported, ADHD. Struggling to keep her head above water whilst balancing the extra demands on executive functioning becoming a mother brings.

So why are women so predisposed to making everyone happy and given such highly tuned intuition and empathy, with or without ADHD?

Survival

If you can read faces and voices, you can tell what a baby needs and sense what a bigger, more aggressive, powerful male is about to do. You can head off any disputes that might mean being thrown out of the tribe and having to hunt, protect and fend for yourself and your young. Women are programmed to keep the peace; we knew we were safer in tribes and would have a greater chance of protecting our young.

Being part of the tribe, although no longer necessary for survival, still feels essential today. Our egos and primal wiring still prioritise fitting in, being popular, liked and accepted. Which for highly sensitive women with ADHD, is exhausting!

We are programmed and socially conditioned to avoid conflict, at home, at work, in the family and with our partner.

The effect is a very physical one. If we think that we are about to lose a relationship, our serotonin, dopamine and oxytocin levels drop, our cortisol levels rise, and we feel under threat. Leaving us feeling anxious, overwhelmed and unable to think about anything else.

For years we swallow our words, stay quiet, sacrifice our happiness, giving up our time and energy in the pursuit of keeping the peace for the sake of protection. Turning ourselves this way and that to keep everyone safe.

Then there are our hormones

Most scientific research still tells us there is little difference between ADHD in men and women, but women who are being diagnosed are living a different story.

How can there not be differences when ADHD is a brain disorder that affects behaviours, and a woman's behaviour is complex due to our emotional brains, greater cultural expectations, social conditioning and fluctuating hormones.

The Berkeley Girls with ADHD Longitudinal Study followed its subjects from childhood to womanhood found that girls with

ADHD have problems that boys don't have, and they are more likely to be overlooked at school and rejected by their peers.

Girls and women with ADHD tend to take their problems out more on themselves than others, creating higher levels of anxiety and depression. If a boy does badly at a test, he is more likely to say, *"stupid test"*, while a girl is more likely to say, *"stupid me"*.

Girls are more prone than boys to self-harm, with high incidences of eating disorders and 1 in 4 making an attempt on their life by the age of twenty. They are also more likely to participate in risky sexual behaviour, with much higher rates of unplanned pregnancies.

Sadly, this vital study is currently paused due to lack of funding, which is a great shame and speaks volumes!

Fluctuating estrogen, progesterone, and testosterone levels affect behaviours, mood and energy, along with cognitive and executive function from puberty to post-menopause and beyond. Research published in the Journal of Psychiatric Research shows that *ADHD*ers are more vulnerable to premenstrual dysphoric disorder (PMDD) and Postnatal Depression.

Estrogen enhances the release of Dopamine and Serotonin. When levels fall during our menstrual cycle, after birth and in peri-post-menopause, ADHD symptoms can worsen.

Puberty is a challenging time to be coping with an invisible disability alongside raging hormones and the social and academic pressure of being a teen. Girls can become more aggressive, withdrawn, reckless, emotional and volatile at this time. Whilst all teenagers can experience these issues and feelings, it is undoubtedly more intense for neurodiverse teens and even more so for girls.

Square Pegs can suffer severe PMT, with ADHD symptoms increasing during the luteal phase as the increase in progesterone diminishes estrogen's calming effects and cognitive support in the last half of the cycle.

Causing significant increases in brain fog, anxiety, indecisiveness and emotional dysregulation.

Unfortunately, many women also report a reduction in ADHD medication effectiveness during this time, when it is needed the most.

Side Note *Try to schedule your month so that you work with your menstrual flow. Doing more challenging, social or focused projects in the first two weeks, the follicular phase when you have more energy to spare, great cognitive ability, and will feel calmer and more sociable. Keeping your diary quieter and less demanding for the last two weeks.*

Post Natal Depression

Studies have proven that incidences of post-natal depression are higher in *ADHD*ers.

Motherhood can be overwhelming for any woman, but the added pressures on a brain already working harder than most and expectations to keep up and be the perfect mum, alongside the drop in estrogen, renders executive functioning non-existent and can push *Square Pegs* into overwhelm and depression.

They may also have stopped taking ADHD medications while pregnant and breastfeeding, removing cognitive support when needed the most.

Women diagnosed later in life often tell me how difficult things were after the birth of their first child. It was the same for me; like so many other times in my life, I thought it was just me being unable to cope.

Menopause

Menopause can be a lonely, scary and confusing time, especially if you don't know you have ADHD or are in menopause.

Our cycles become more erratic, and PMT can come at any point in the month. Women report having one good week and three bad at this later stage.

Think of puberty in reverse without the teenage angst of fitting in, spots and who's going out with who; now we have big girl problems, bills to pay, families to look after and careers to shine in, all whilst our estrogen levels are swinging from high to low daily, like a light switch turning on and off.

The average age of menopause in the UK is fifty-one, with most women starting to feel the symptoms about three to four years prior. The ovaries will have stopped producing estrogen by the age of sixty, and most menopause symptoms should be under control by then. However, if you are one of the few for whom this is not the case, then speak with your GP because HRT could still be an option. No woman needs to go through hell.

Menopause is the twenty-hour hours, 365 after your last period that marks the end of our menstrual cycle and a large decline in our oestrogen. Leading up to that the Peri-menopause, starts as early as thirty-five, although you aren't likely to notice any effects until your early forties, when you may notice your periods start to change, often becoming more frequent and sometimes heavier in these early days unless you are in early menopause, which can happen at any age.

Because of the rollercoaster of fluctuating hormones testing to see if you are in menopause is pretty useless as results vary daily. As you get closer to menopause, your periods should start to get further apart, less heavy and shorter in most cases. This and age are two signs you are nearing menopause. I suggest using an App to track your period and cycle length and using it as a monthly check to see how things are.

Side note *Birth control is important throughout this time because the closer you get to menopause, the less sure you can be as to when you are ovulating, so take heed.*

In these peri-menopausal years, a *Square Pegs* foot to the floor, stressful lifestyle can start to catch up, as all women naturally become less resilient and so struggle to keep all the *balls in the air.*

Menopausal symptoms such as low energy, brain fog, hot flushes, night sweats, emotional outbursts, and difficulties maintaining a healthy weight, even for those exercising, are all exacerbated by stress.

Brain fog can be scary for women of this age, and many tell me they'd questioned if they had the start of something more sinister such as Alzheimer's.

Dr Lisa Mosconi has a fantastic TED talk on this subject; her work on the female brain during menopause is groundbreaking. She says between the ages of forty-three and fifty-one (peri-post menopausal) women can get a 30% reduction in brain energy, but things usually return to normal after menopause, although this is a new normal."

Side Note *ADHD symptoms and menopause can look very similar, and one could be mistaken for the other. If your ADHD symptoms have only been present or an issue since your peri-menopause, it may be* *that causing the symptoms rather than ADHD. If it's ADHD, you can trace problems throughout your life.*

I am a strong advocate for body-identical HRT when the natural strategies need a helping hand, as is Dr Mosconi and many other leading doctors and researchers.

HRT helped me at forty-eight when I struggled with menopausal and ADHD symptoms. Within just a few weeks, both had significantly improved.

Available on the NHS, Body Identical HRT is made from yams, mimics your body's estrogen, and is easily absorbed through the skin.

If you want to know more about the latest research and information on HRT, you can find articles under the blog section of my website over at https://kimrainecoaching.com/blog/.

Side Note If you are struggling with any of the above, there is help; speak with someone you trust, or join a support group or charity on or offline where you can open up. If you feel that you may have undiagnosed ADHD, then see your GP, armed with a list of symptoms and evidence dating back to your childhood, so you can advocate for yourself and push hard for a diagnosis. This is not you; it is your brain, it needs some help, and that's ok.

Whilst ADHD makes all of these times harder; there are things we can do to lessen the symptoms. These areas are:

- Cortisol Regulation - managing and minimising our stress.
- Circadian rhythm disruption - prioritising our sleep.
- Blood sugar dis-regulation - optimising nutrition, exercise and lifestyle choices

- Inflammation - gut health, lifestyle and the chemical load we put on our bodies.

We will discuss these as part of your natural high strategies later in this book.

Tune In

What parts of this section have resonated with you the most?

How do you think your female brain wiring and hormones effects your life?

What are your takeaways from this chapter, and what can you put in place to help you now?

4

THE EMOTIONAL ROLLERCOASTER

Square Pegs are sensitive people, physically and emotionally. Thanks to highly sensitive nervous systems, they can have disabling hypersensitivities to noise, smells, lighting or other aspects in the environment, such as textures, lights, colours, temperatures, flavours, smells and technology;

How do you feel about noisy chewing?

I cannot eat a meal in silence as the noise of others chewing feels unbearable.

Sensitivity to clothing, tags, labels and touch, especially soft, can feel extremely uncomfortable for some

Tactile hypersensitivity to light touch is not uncommon, especially in women. It is something I have struggled with and has caused me much confusion and guilt over the years, as the two people who triggered me most were two of my dearest people, my Mum and my husband. It makes sense now, I know, because most other people don't touch me tenderly. There was someone else who used to touch me softly when she greeted me, a kiss always accompanied it. I used to feel on edge just walking towards her as I knew what was coming!

Their gentle touch would set my skin on fire, and it seemed to get worse, or I was more aware of it as I got older. Discovering that we can be so sensitive to touch was a relief to read and I showed my husband immediately. Up until then, I had never been able to explain it; I'd react by jumping out of my skin and biting his head off every time he came near me.

I am much better with firmer touch, like a hug from my children that fills me full of Oxytocin.

I struggle at dusk too; I need to have the lights on as the natural dimness of the light makes me feel highly agitated.

How about you? Do you have any sensitivities that you thought were a bit strange and over the top, hopefully until now?

We are also highly sensitive to energy.

I am very sensitive to others' energy, especially in my personal space. I can't cope with people standing too close or reading over my shoulder. I could never figure out why it was such an issue, and at times it was an issue.

I used to avoid my favourite butchers if the owner, who was a lovely man, was there, as he couldn't help invading my space, so much so I blurted out to him, *"this is my space, that's yours"*, one day, I covered it up with a joke, but we both knew I'd just lost it a little bit!

Managing Emotions

This extreme sensitivity is the reason for what can be one of the most embarrassing elements for any *Square Peg* who struggles to put the breaks on their emotions, good or bad, emotional outbursts.

Emotional dysregulation is when our inability to modulate or manage strong emotions spirals, and we react in an inappropriate or over-the-top way, internally or publicly.

Super sensitivity can mean misinterpreting signals or intentions, leading to overreactions, saying regrettable things or lashing out. This inability to react appropriately can cause us to be even more sensitive and likely to overreact when we feel emotions we have experienced in the past rising within us. The sheer fear of our response to that emotion can cause us to act before the issue has even arisen, all of which is happening at a subconscious level, meaning our reactions can be as much of a shock to us as it is to others and leaving us feeling deeply remorseful later.

In some cases, the intensity of the emotion, good or bad, can become so overwhelming we shut down. Dr Tom Brown calls this Emotional Flooding, which he describes as,

> *"An extended period of intense emotion that shuts the person down, so they struggle to function at all."*

Episodes like these take time to get over.

One of my clients recently had to spend a very stressful eight hours in A&E with her three-year-old daughter. The lighting, the people, the noise, the boredom and the stress of keeping her daughter occupied left her feeling highly sensitive and emotional. Luckily kind nursing staff found her a room after she burst into tears about five hours in. She said she spent the next day unable to engage or speak to anyone as the intense effort it took to keep control of her emotions had exhausted her.

Square Pegs are generally pretty easy-going, fun people to be around. However, when they feel pressured, frustrated or trapped in some way and it collides with their impulsivity, they can explode in a flash of intense emotion that shocks themselves and those around them. In some cases, the consequences can be dire, especially in teens.

It is estimated that 70% of first-time juvenile offenders have ADHD.

When we experience such intense emotional feelings, the Amygdala hijacks the brain, putting us straight into fight or flight, instantly shutting down our ability to access the executive functioning we need to make calm, rational decisions and think straight.

How do you react to the stress in your life?

When we feel under threat or a perceived threat, such as a stressful situation, conversation, confrontation, or event, our bodies' first line of response is the alarm phase. The brain goes in to act now think later mode, releases the hormones you need, and we automatically react in one of three primal ways. Fight, flight or freeze.

You will have felt this life-saving response many times when you slam the brakes on in an emergency stop, pull your hand away from a hot oven, jump out of your skin during a horror film, or when you're walking down a dodgy street at night.

People who are stressed, have suffered trauma, and are struggling with anxiety or have ADHD can find this response gets over-triggered and exaggerated, causing the nervous system to become easily activated.

Each of the three F's has a different response; which one do you think is your most common go-to response?

Are you a fighter? Immediately diving in to protect yourself, meeting fire with fire, threatening or reacting with an aggressive response, often blowing up and overacting. Saying terrible things, shouting or snapping.

Or do you flee, doing everything in your power to escape the situation. Flight is often the response when we perceive the threat to be more than we can handle. This can be walking out of an intense situation, avoiding a difficult conversation or hiding away.

What about freeze? This response is all about overwhelm; you are so overwhelmed by the perceived threat you can't respond; think deer in the headlights. Your brain shuts down, and instead of letting your feelings and emotions out, you stuff them down to fester, ready to explode later.

Becoming more aware of how you respond to these situations gives you the space to explore how you would like to respond to these situations. With attention, work and practice, it is possible to slow your response down long enough to act consciously instead.

I also used to be a fighter, my first line of defence was always attack.

There are times that I have reacted in fight, that I deeply regret. I see how it damaged my relationships which, although they survived the storm, the fact is once you react to someone that way, you have triggered their threat response, meaning, they will have laid down their own warning system that says you're dangerous and to tread carefully.

Be honest, do you want people treading carefully around you? I knew I didn't!

Meditation and how I manage my day-to-day stress and commitments has been a real game changer in helping me change my threat response; it enabled me to slow things down and think before reacting. I take confrontation, criticism and pressure much better now.

Dealing with criticism or rejection

Research has proven that we feel pain more intensely and for longer than most neurotypicals which can lead to us holding on to old hurts for years, forever analysing and reliving conversations and events, thus keeping the pain alive.

Rejection Sensitivity Dysphoria can affect anyone but is very common in *ADHD*ers, many of the women I work with resonate instantly when we talk about it.

Everybody fears rejection; we all care what others think, but with RSD, the response is often overwhelming and all-consuming. People with RSD have a paralysing fear of rejection that can produce an extreme emotional response.

Negative feedback, comments, judgement or exclusion, perceived or actual, can send *Square Pegs* into a painful and paralysing loop of negative thoughts and deep hurt that can last years. RSD is more prevalent in females, which shouldn't surprise you now you know that we are neurologically and physiologically designed to be more in touch with our emotions than our male counterparts.

Many *Square Pegs* suffer repeated rejection, exclusion and humiliation from friends, family, colleagues and teachers as they struggle to navigate a neurotypical world, often in silence and undiagnosed. Due to their high sensitivity, what others see as teasing or having fun can feel like deeply hurtful criticism or nastiness to them.

RSD can flair up in a second, leaving the feeling of overwhelming fixation on the negative emotion. A flippant comment, overlooked invitation, or facial expression can quickly turn to depression, anger, rage, bitterness or isolation and years of sleepless nights replaying and analysing old hurts.

It can show up in relationships and friendships with women finding themselves being badly treated but staying because the fear of abandonment or rejection is too great. Or stop them from making any effort to have anyone in their life, all because the safest way to avoid the intense emotional pain of rejection is not to try to be successful, loved or liked.

Square Pegs who struggle with RSD are often perfectionists. However, they would never think that themselves because they continually feel that nothing they do is ever good enough, living in fear of being found out, exposed or rejected. To avoid this rejection, they are prone to people pleasing too, having few or low boundaries that they allow others to push, struggling to say no or taking on more than their fair share of the workload.

RSD is exhausting.

Perfectionism

I can always spot a perfectionist; they say things like,

> *"Me? No way, I'm not a perfectionist."*

> *"I just need to add this last bit."*

"It was nowhere near as good as...."

Perfectionism stems from the underlying feelings of shame and low self-confidence that exacerbates ADHD challenges and ignites a constant need to do more.

Remember, it's also a sneaky form of procrastination that you must watch out for; the need to be perfectly ready before starting a task can mean the task never gets started. Especially if the fear of not hitting the high standard you set for yourself leaves you stuck in constant planning or inaction.

When I have a client that does every bit of homework, is always early and wants to get everything right, I know anxiety isn't far away.

A lady on one of my programmes was a self-confessed perfectionist, which hugely affected her life. She was feeling overwhelmed with the need for everything to be perfect. She said she craved praise, always wanted to be the best and was petrified of failure. One day on a call, we had a breakthrough when she realised how exhausting having such high expectations and never feeling good enough or able to keep up was.

High expectations can lead to feelings of failure, let down and unhappiness that isn't just of yourself but others too.

One of the world's greatest footballers, Cristiano Ronaldo, says he strives for excellence, not perfection: *'I am not a perfectionist, but I like to feel that things are done well.'*

This makes far more sense; aim to be excellent, not perfect.

Menopause and ageing can reduce perfectionism. That magical time of life when the hormones that have made us give so much of a crap about what people think start to diminish, leaving us older, wiser, and more aware that perfection is an impossible destination, and its pursuit is exhausting.

Mistakes are good things, and so is failing. It is how we learn and how we grow.

In the gym, there is only one way to get stronger, and that is to fail. Keep lifting heavier and heavier until you fail; that is your threshold for growth and strength.

Are you afraid to fail? Don't be, it is a vital part of mastery and excellence. Failure is the path to improvement.

When I used to be a rather naff snowboarder, I would love the days I completed without crashing down on my coccyx or my knees, they were good days, but the truth was they were the days I stayed the same. The days my knees were bruised, and my butt was killing me were the days I improved, which came only by failing repeatedly.

Overthinking

All brains love to ruminate, but our superfast, hyperactive ADHD brain slips into rumination more easily than most, with females having been proven to ruminate more than men.

Ruminating is giving our problems continuous attention, feeding and watering them so that they grow like anything fed and watered.

It's linked to depression, anxiety, PTSD, addiction and self-soothing behaviours such as emotional eating or excessive drinking.

Studies show that people who ruminate less have lower levels of anxiety and depression.

We use ruminating to problem solve and protect ourselves by retracing our past situations or events to ensure better future outcomes. Still, it can become like listening to a stuck record rather than solving the problem. You can find yourself repeatedly going over should of, would of, could of, filling your head with negative self talk and criticism, blaming and berating others or ourselves for everything and feeling stuck in a miserable cycle, replaying conversations, arguments, events, heartbreak and grief.

Carrying these thoughts around all the time dampens our energy, leaving us feeling drained, emotional and unable to get going. A result of all the worrying, lying awake at night and feeling hopeless or just passing through our days constantly thinking of hurts and problems.

The Default Mode Network and Negativity Bias

When our mind is freely wandering, such as daydreaming, something our busy and creative minds love to do, we engage our *Default Mode Network.*

The DMN moves fast, approx 300-1000 words a minute and only about a third of that time is positive or happy; the other two-thirds are neutral, stressful or negative.

It has been proven that around 80% of the worries and fears the brain comes up with during rumination will never materialise or be anywhere near as disastrous as the scenarios in your head.

The reason our ruminating is so often on the bad rather than the good is that our brains are hardwired for negativity. Scientists call this our *negativity bias,* which is an important part of our survival. Without it, we would do stupid things, jump on the road, sit in fires, etc.

It keeps us safe and allows us to process life-saving negative thoughts and experiences a lot faster and more thoroughly than positive ones. In order to create this safely reference library, our negative experiences stay with us for longer.

A mindfulness teacher once described this to me using Teflon and Velcro.

Negative comments and experiences stick to the brain like Velcro, whilst the compliments and the good times bounce off as if it is Teflon coated.

When we have a bad experience, our Amygdala, the area of our brain that stores negative memories away for our protection and kick starts our 3 F's, Fight, Flight or Freeze, fires up to ensure our survival, whether that is on the road or in the boardroom.

Its job is to constantly check for negative situations or possibilities. two-thirds of the neurons in this part of the brain are geared towards negativity, always ready to scan for threats, especially things that have threatened us in the past and might be a threat to us again.

The survival system that we have used for thousands of years to protect us has now become our enemy as our lives are no longer as dangerous, yet we are still looking for it all the time.

DMN activates our daydreams, memories and random thoughts when the mind is at rest. These thoughts can be negative, or they can be positive.

Random thoughts, like *"what did she really mean by that"* *"I don't like sausages"*, *"how does she manage to do that?"*, *"did he look at me funny"* *"what shall we do at the weekend"*...you know the sort of thing!

It is greatly affected by our state of mind. If you are in a positive frame of mind or have a positive outlook on life, then your DMN can be a cool and creative place to hang out. A place where the *Square Pegs* brain can come into its own, coming up with solutions and ideas that are truly ingenious.

But if you constantly ruminate over your past or worry about the future, you will struggle with an overactive Amygdala and a head full of negativity.

We will talk more later about this, but for now, if you know you often dig up the past, then a great way to calm an overactive DMN is to practise gratitude and mindfulness, to bring yourself into the moment wherever you are.

At your desk, in traffic, or a meeting, you can concentrate on your breathing, the feel of the steering wheel, your back in the seat, and the feeling as you relax your shoulders and release the tension from your jaw, and nobody needs to know.

Just focusing on that particular moment, not judging or criticising, just noticing and observing.

Doing this engages the *Task Positive Network* (TPN), which in most of the population inhabits the DMN, making it dormant, i.e., you are in the moment concentrating on the task, switching off the daydreaming and giving you a pause to change your mental state.

However, in the ADHD brain, the on/off switch between these two is less effective, maybe even absent in some, which is one of the reasons scientists believe we find transitioning from one task to another or staying focused so challenging, especially when we are doing things that bore us.

Next time you catch yourself negatively ruminating, try switching gears and focus by doing something that fully engages your brain and fires up the *Task Positive Network* to at least lessen the rumination.

Start to become more aware of your thoughts and notice when your DMN is taking over and do something you love instead, like calling a friend, going for a walk, practicing a hobby or putting on a favourite tune.

The best way I know to shift from the DMN to the TPN is breathing. I use rescue breathes to tone down my parasympathetic nervous system and help me to relax.

Breathe in for the count of four, hold it for seven, breathe out for eight and repeat for a few rounds.

We will discuss this and the power of pausing later when we dive deeper into strategies.

The more you practise using things like mindfulness and gratitude to change your state when you're feeling down or negative, the more you will see your thoughts as simple occurrences in the mind, passing like clouds rather than needing to be addressed or engaged with and the happier and less negative you will become.

Sidenote Did you know music is the quickest way to change an emotion? I get all my clients to create a feel-good playlist to help fire them up and refocus them when they are struggling to focus or in a negative mood.

Tune In

What parts resonated with you the most?

Are you hypersensitive? What triggers you.

Can you walk into a room and immediately pick up on the atmosphere and an individual's feelings?

How would you describe your DMN? Would it be primarily positive, neutral or negative?

How can you use what you have learned to help you better manage your emotions?

What are your takeaways from this chapter, and what can you put in place to help you now?

5

IT'S NOT YOUR FAULT, BUT IT IS YOUR RESPONSIBILITY

There are times when ADHD is exhausting, life can feel like walking through treacle, but the truth is no one is coming to save you and whilst our neurodivergent brains aren't our fault, they are our responsibility, and there is much we can do to make vast improvements.

This next section is about doing just that; we will start reexamining the stories, self-talk and beliefs you have developed from a life of undiagnosed ADHD. When you assumed everyone's brain was like yours and that you either didn't fit in, needed to try harder or weren't enough.

Buckle up as some of these following chapters might be challenging, but they are the essence of self-discovery and an essential part of your journey.

Acknowledging where you are right now is a powerful and sometimes difficult start to a journey of self-discovery, but taking responsibility and holding yourself accountable puts you rather than your ADHD in the driving seat of your life...more of the time!

You must be honest and face the truth about how you got here. It is time to sort the facts from the fiction. It can be one of those ouch moments that can leave you feeling angry and resentful about all of the time you have wasted at the mercy of undiagnosed ADHD.

There will be things in your life where you know your ADHD got the better of you or you feel others let you down, there is only one way to deal with that, and it's with compassion. You and they were doing the best with the skills and information available at the time.

You are where you are, and that's ok. The fact that you are taking ownership is a good sign that you are well on your way to success. Acknowledging your neurodiverse brain and the reality you are in is an exciting place to be.

From victim to victor

As a youngster, I never took ownership of any of my problems. I saw myself as helpless and blameless. I would use excuses and bob along in whatever direction life would take me, waiting to see where I'd end up next.

Allowing myself to think like that put me in victim mode and left me at the mercy of fate and others. The day I realised no one was coming to save me was when I started to take ownership of my problems and control of my destiny; it was exciting and empowering.

I felt quite grown up, like I had a handle on the *adulting* many of my peers had been doing for years.

When things didn't go my way, I started to ask myself what had gone wrong and the part I had played, which meant I could learn lessons for a better outcome in the future.

Although it might seem overwhelming taking responsibility for our lives is the most empowering thing we can do. It instantly puts us in control of our destiny and allows us to sort our crap out.

The sooner we realise that no one is coming to save us, the quicker we can start doing something about the situation ourselves.

Where is your focus?

Getting out of your way and taking ownership greatly impacts your life. Taking that all-important pause to ask where you spend your time and energy at any given moment can take you from victim mode to power ON mode. If things are never your fault and you are always blaming and complaining, you are reacting, waiting for someone or something to save you, but the truth is, with that attitude, you will forever struggle to achieve your true potential.

I remember the moment I realised my attitude was holding me back from getting where I wanted.

It hit me like a slap in the face when Darren, one of my first mentors, pointed out how negative I was, which, if you knew me now, you would never believe. I have been told on more than one occasion I am annoyingly positive.

I was working at the European Institute of Fitness, training students to become Personal Trainers. Darren was my boss, and I thought he was amazing. I had never met anyone so constantly positive and upbeat in my life. It was the best job in the world, but I must have been moaning about something that *Wasn't my fault* or feeling sorry for myself because he turned around to me and said,*"Kim, how come the cup is always half empty with you."*

It struck me like a bolt of lightning; he was right. I always looked at the negative side of things. Whenever there was a problem, I would allow myself to be entirely overtaken by it, spiralling down into the worst possible scenario, blaming everyone or thing else and completely disempowering myself from being able to find a solution.

This was one of those moments when you suddenly have a shift in perspective that changes your life.

I began to change; it wasn't easy. There were thirty years of programming to undo, but the first stage of any change is awareness, and so with this new perspective, I began to make changes to the way I thought.

Whenever I heard myself blaming or complaining, I would switch my perspective and flip that thought to look for the positive, the lesson or the solution rather than the problem.

The *blaming and complaining cycle* is a low-energy place to live where you will always be at the mercy of the challenge and at a level of conciseness where it is virtually impossible to find solutions. Living with this mindset wastes one of your strongest talents because our ingenious brains excel in problem-solving.

Explanation or excuse?

Making excuses is another disempowering habit to be aware of. Yes to compassion and understanding, but endless excuses, no.

There are times when we all make excuses. When we've had a bad run of it, and it all seems unfair, it can feel good and possibly necessary to wallow for a while, but then it's time to pick ourselves up, dust ourselves off and start taking action. My friends say I am getting my guns out when I'm like this, which basically means enough of the pity party, time to face the truth and take action.

This is typical ADHD behaviour; we are doers and action takers.

If you want to make progress and live the life you deserve, then excuses and sob stories will get you nowhere. I'm a big fan of mantras, positive psychology and manifesting but not as much as I believe in getting off your bum and taking action, big or small, towards your daily goals. You will never have the best possible life, health, relationship, bank account or anything by simply wishing for it.

From now on, I want you to check yourself, notice when you are making excuses, blaming and complaining; how does it feel?

Do you feel powerful or powerless?

Take a pause, flip that thought and step into solution-based problem solving. Take ownership and ask what you can do to solve the problem.

Tune In

What parts of this chapter have resonated with you the most?

Where do you spend most of your time and energy?

Do you blame, complain and make excuses or do you take responsibility?

How can you use what you have just learned to help you flip your mindset and take more responsibility?

What are your takeaways from this chapter, and what can you put in place to help you now?

6

WILL THE REAL YOU PLEASE STAND UP

Women describe getting an ADHD diagnosis as a relief. Realising that certain parts of their persona are nothing to do with them is a revelation.

ADHD affects our thoughts, feelings and behaviours, so it is no wonder that many of the women I work with have no idea who they are after years of living undiagnosed, keeping everyone else happy and putting themselves last on the list.

How often have you said or thought, *I am happy… if everyone else is happy*?

We've talked about the sacrifices a woman can make over the years whilst trying to find room for herself, but often there has been no time for that self.

Kids, work, managing teams, running businesses, bosses, employees, being taxis, cheerleaders, playing so many different roles all needing new energy and personalities. Is it any wonder we can find ourselves skidding into mid-life thinking…

- *Who the hell am I?*
- *What do I want?*

When you know who you are and you have a purpose that plays to your interests and strengths, life is good. Finding purpose can get you out of bed with a spring in your step each day and bring even the most traumatised human back from despair.

So how about you, do you know who you are and what you want? Or does it just feel like a big jumble that is easier forgotten about as the days go by?

Are you in flow?

When you are in flow life feels so much easier, everything from getting out of bed to doing the dishes feels easier, we need interest to get us going.

Living an unfulfilling life is like ADHD kryptonite.

Some of the signs you might see when you are off course are:

- You live in fight or flight
- You feel anxious
- Your energy is low
- You can't sleep
- You aren't showing up in business
- You can't focus or move forward
- You don't act like yourself around certain people or situations
- You are self-medicating with whatever it is you use
- You feel moody, down and your days disappear into a vortex of procrastination and menial tasks

The above are all challenges our ADHD brain can throw at us at anytime, but when you are feeling disconnected and lost these challenges become more and more frequent, leaving you wondering who the person in the mirror is.

Influenced by our people pleasing brains we shape and mould ourselves into what we think will help us fit in the best, even doing it to our children too, desperate for them to fit in to societies round hole #guilty.

Our identities are our strength and our power, they are the true essence of who we are and we should make every effort to ensure that we are honouring our authentic square peg selves rather than trying to fit in to societies round holes at all times.

It is time to take off the mask and be your true self.

A client said to me the other day, *"I am think since being diagnosed I have become more ADHD"*

I have seen this in myself and others too.

I don't think it is about becoming more ADHD. I think it comes from spending less time and energy trying to mirror our neurotypical peers, becoming more ourselves, and less afraid of letting the world see a little bit more of who we truly are.

To find your true identity, you need to unpick the values, stories, beliefs and experiences that have led you to this point. It is no easy feat as there are so many factors to consider.

We become comfortable with our stories, even if we know them to be untrue. We form habits, beliefs and traits to help us feel physically and emotionally safe, but they can leave us with tunnel vision, stuck in fight or flight & skewing our perception of what's possible.

Unless you recalibrate, you will be stuck in a state where thoughts can run wild, your emotions are all over the show, and you feel powerless to change.

As a *Square Peg* you might have learnt to doubt your voice, your internal compass and intuition. You may have lost your identity after years of mirroring others' behaviours and unwittingly using them to guide your decisions and opinions.

It is time to start listening to what's inside of you and what you want. Lean into the discomfort of not always being nice. Get comfortable risking backlash to follow your internal compass rather than doing what others expect of you, or more often what you think others expect of you.

Follow your heart.

Use your voice!

Being your true self can take bravery and courage which is why it is always helpful to have a strong sense of your values, the things that are important to you.

Values

We all have personal values that drive our decision-making processes, think of it as your likes and dislikes in their basic form. We pick them up from our peers, events, cultures, beliefs, environments and significant people in our lives. They are passed down in families from generation to generation like heirlooms.

All of this means that the values you hold so dear may not even be your own, yet they will be having a big influence on you.

Values drive the decisions and behaviours that govern how we live our lives. Knowing what our values are cannot only help us make decisions they can show us who we are and why we sometimes struggle to make the right decisions, especially if those decisions are more about what others want, than what we want or need.

Decisions are one of those ADHD polarities, sometimes we are great decisions makers, other times deciding what shoes to wear exhausts us!

When your values are clear to you it makes decisions a lot easier.

The first time I did a deep dive into my values was back in 2018 following a conversation with my coach about my business at the time.

I ran a series of female fitness camps in Surrey, and it was fantastic. The community of women we had all created was second to none, we supported each other through divorces, weddings, births, bereavements, cancers, personal achievements and more. I loved it. It was everything to me.

However, the stories I was privy to and the insights I was having behind the scenes of these women's lives left me wanting to work with them at a much deeper level than the camp environment allowed.

My online coaching business was growing, and I was feeling torn, I felt I couldn't do both well and I could see I wasn't able to facilitate the permanent changes in the women's lives I wanted too through the camps anymore.

I felt lost, I wasn't sleeping and I wasn't giving the camps my all.

I spoke with my coach about the genuine turmoil I was in, and we decided to take a look at my true values.

As I worked through the exercises it became clear what I needed to do in the best interest of myself and the community, and that was to sell the business and hand over the baton to someone who could continue the journey.

It was a really tough decision to make but as I dived deeper and deeper into what was important to me I knew I need to get on a different path. I know that this one exercise changed everything for me and allowed me to do the transformative work I do with women today.

These are the values that I still use to guide me today.

FREEDOM

Freedom is so important to me.

- The freedom to be your authentic self and live your truth.
- The freedom to say what you want and be who and how you are.
- The freedom to go and explore, experiment and have an adventure.
- The freedom to fail.

STAGE

- Stage is about being proud of who you are.
- Holding your space.
- Speaking up.
- Being bold and brave.
- Being heard.
- Owning your shiz and speaking your truth.

CONNECTION

- With family, friends and strangers.
- Offering love, understanding and support.
- Having fun.
- Being kind at every opportunity.
- Laughing and laughing and laughing.
- Filling your days full of smiles, giggles and kindness.

What are your values?

Stop now and list everything that is important to you.

Thinking about this can be tough if you are feeling lost and disconnected so let me give you some prompts to journal on.

Just let the pen say what it wants.

Answer these questions in as much detail as you can, the more description the better.

- *What does your perfect day look like?*
- *What times and things are you most proud of in your life?*
- *When do you feel most alive?*
- *What really F's you off?*
- *What are you willing to fight for?*

Now take the top five things that matter most.

If your value is family first, when faced with a decision the immediate unconscious consideration is will this affect my family?

If it's success the thought will be will this make me more or less successful?

But what about when the decision will make you more successful but affect your family dynamics, what happens then?

Sometimes our values can cause us conflict.

Family vs Success

Friends vs Giving up alcohol

Partner vs Life goals

Putting them in order of importance will reduce conflict and enable better decision making.

Now, go back to your list of five and put them in order of importance.

I have worked with many women whose values are conflicting, often family vs work. This is when you need a firm set of very simple rules and boundaries to protect and honour both values. Understanding what is really important to you can help you reset your internal compass, putting you back on the right track.

Having this list of 3-5 words that incapsulate the essence of who you are and what you stand for means you can quickly check in and see if the decisions you are making are in alignment with your core values or not.

Now look at the areas of your life, such as work, home, relationships, friendships, and ask are these in alignment with my values?

If you're struggling with this exercise here are some of the ones my clients have come up with after taking a deep dive on one of my programmes or at a workshop.

- Faith
- Wisdom

- Harmony
- Freedom
- Unity
- Wholehearted
- Balance
- Peace
- Connection
- Wellbeing
- Creation
- Home
- Grounding
- Empowerment
- Adventure

Now I want you to use your creative ADHD brain to bring them to life.

Make a vision board with pictures to show what's important to you, or a mind map full of colour and life.

These words are your guide so have them visible and at the forefront of your mind so that when our impulsive, live in the moment bouncy brains take you off on an adventure or are struggling to make a decision you can take that all important pause and ask if what you're doing aligns with what's important to you.

Tune In

What has resonated with you most in this chapter?

Can you see where you might having been living according to the values of others?

Now you have an idea of what's most important to you ask yourself these questions for each value.

How do I honour this?

Am I honouring it right now?

How can I honour it even more?

What are your takeaways from this chapter and what can you put in place to help you now?

7

WHAT'S YOU, WHAT'S ADHD, AND WHAT'S THE TRUTH?

Understanding how your brain works and applying the strategies that work with your brain rather than against it is an invaluable step towards a phenomenal life.

ADHD wasn't generally diagnosed in adults until the 1990's and even then, it was mostly the hyperactive types with the more common inattentive types still flying way under the radar.

So I am guessing that if you are reading this then like me you were a little late to the party.

Meaning you have accumulated a lifetime of beliefs and stories based around trying to keep up and fit in.

Undiagnosed ADHD results in poor educational outcomes, career challenges, relationship issues, higher probability of drug and alcohol addiction, seriously damaged self-esteem, lack of financial security, the list goes on, and all of it shapes the stories we tell ourselves.

These stories, that are based on challenges, negative experiences and the belief that we should be able to do better can keep us locked in negative situations and sitting on the sidelines watching life pass us by.

Our stories and beliefs are down to our model of the world and govern how we see life. No two people see life totally the same, we all have our own unique experiences of life and it's the lessons we take from them that shape us and form the beliefs, opinions and reality that become our stories

Once we have these stories and beliefs, we automatically look for evidence to uphold our perception of reality, each time adding to the layers that reinforces the belief.

We form much of our belief systems in childhood when we are in a non-analytical alpha state. We are like sponges constantly soaking up the information around us, downloading our programming and creating our unique view of the world, made from a mixture of our experiences and the beliefs of family, peers and teachers. Later these beliefs help form our values.

Later in life we form beliefs in other environments, our peer groups, partners, colleagues and organisations.

Our beliefs, can make or break us

It is estimated that the typical ADHD child experiences a devastating half a MILLION negative, coercive or oppositional interactions every year! Every one of those experiences will be a layer of negative belief, that shapes our ability to succeed.

The main reasons people don't achieve their goals are:

- *They have limiting beliefs*

- *They doubt their capabilities*
- *They get scared of succeeding.*
- *They don't believe it.*

One of the biggest reasons that women fail at anything is that they don't believe that they are capable of doing it.

I used to run a programme called *Slim from Within* for women who had tried everything to lose weight. The women who joined felt hopeless. They had collected so much evidence from previous failed attempts that losing weight was impossible for them, they had built themselves a cast iron story that nothing would work.

Only 20% of what we talked about was strategy (nutrition and exercise in this case), the rest was all mindset, stories and beliefs.

They had limiting beliefs, based on previous failed attempts and experiences. They doubted themselves and their ability, feeling almost silly for believing anything else was possible, no one likes to feel a failure so many people don't even bother to try and be anything else.

This programme was such fun for me to run because I only had to make them change their beliefs to get them great results.

As they started to lose weight their belief in themselves and their success would grow and as it did their whole identity would start to shift as they started to take more and more actions that would take them closer to their goal. Over a short period of time, they stopped hitting snooze, got out of bed and to the gym.

They started seeing that one unhealthy meal didn't mean you had failed and just got back on with eating well.

You will never transform your life until you change the stories you tell yourself and the beliefs around it.

Your belief about the outcome of whatever you are going to do has a big impact on whether you will take action or not. As your beliefs change so will your behaviours - you will start taking more positive action towards your goals.

What stories do you tell yourself?

What are the messages that pop up in your head when you try to do something out of your comfort zone or something that you know you have failed at in the past, *which was most likely because you weren't doing it a square peg way!*

What does the little voice, that wants you to stay in the safety of your comfort zone say?

- *That won't work*
- *They'll think I'm stupid*
- *They don't like me*
- *I don't belong there*
- *I'm not good enough to do that.*
- *I'm too busy.*
- *I'm too tired.*
- *I'll look like an idiot.*

And bang, you are frozen, the idea gets shelved and you carry on plodding in the same direction.

But what if you squished that voice before it had the chance to wake.

What if you thought:

- *Who am I not to do this?*
- *I know how my brain works now,*

- *I can use everything I have learnt before and make it happen.*
- *What the worst that can happen?*

How do you think this would change the outcome, what do you think you would feel like doing next?

Taking action, or hitting snooze?

The key here is to move slowly out of your comfort zone and into your stretch zone where you take small but consistent action, gradually increasing your comfort zone, rather than shooting out of it like Roadrunner, only to look down halfway over the cliff and plummet to the ground.

As you take action and start celebrating even a small amount of success you are taking steps to start changing your beliefs and the stories you subconsciously tell yourself about your worth and abilities.

The stories you tell yourself are based on your history and your family history...which may have years of undiagnosed ADHD and co-existing mental health issues running through it.

However, the real story is the facts of the case, everything else you add is perception. Once you understand that you can begin to change the stories, because your story only defines you if you let it!

It's not the events in our lives that shape us it is how we react to them.

Up until now you may have felt unable to control your reactions to challenging events as your ADHD brain literally hijacks your Amygdala and causes you to react in an overly emotional way or shut down completely, depending on the story script at the time.

You can blame your ADHD, late diagnosis, your upbringing, schooling, the government, your environment, your partner, *insert challenge here*, for your situation but it will only drag you down and hold you back. If you can change the stories you tell and learn to take a pause, you will be able to approach events from a more solution focused perspective.

It is our ability to approach these events with a rational perspective that determines our success in any area of life.

Even now if you know you have reacted to a certain situation badly or ineffectively in the past you can still make changes, if not to the outcome at least to the story you are telling yourself.

Let me share the best illustration of this I have ever heard.

Same life, different stories

Identical twin boys, raised together by an alcoholic father.

One is tee total.

One is an alcoholic.

When asked why he doesn't drink the tee-total twin replied, *"because my father was an alcoholic."*

When asked why he was an alcoholic the second twin replied, *"because my father was an alcoholic."*

One set of facts, two very different reactions, stories and beliefs.

Maybe you feel you have stories and beliefs that are just too ingrained to change, even years later you find yourself ruminating and going over and over them.

The injustice feels too great to forgive, let go and move on from.

What's the truth?

But are those stories even true? Is your perception of events factually, correct?

All the stories we tell ourselves are distorted, based on our own internal representation of an external experience, different thoughts, feelings, ideas and opinions.

Our faster than lightening brains take in phenomenal amount of information per second. To make this process super-fast and conserve bandwidth the brain has a gatekeeper, sitting in our subconscious mind called the *Reticular Activation System* RAS, who is automatically filtering out anything it doesn't think is important.

These filters are created from your past experiences, feelings, emotions, perception, decisions, habits and beliefs.

Your RAS will delete, distort and generalise information to tell you what it is it thinks you want to hear, based on what you have been paying attention to.

It's the reason when you decide to buy a yellow mini, suddenly every other car is a yellow mini, the RAS is hunting out what it thinks you want to see.

The subconscious is always trying to protect us and so it will misrepresent the reality of situations. Deleting vital bits of data and making generalisations so we end up with the view that fits in with the story we are telling ourselves.

We make all of our decisions based on these filters, many of which aren't even a true representation of the facts as we recall them.

Memories are subject to contamination, especially for *ADHD*ers who have limitations with working memory.

Scientists believe that every time we recall an event, we need to re-piece the information together, leaving us open to misinformation as we remember the scenarios based on our internal interpretation of it. This interpretation can further change depending on our current reality and influences.

In one study Cognitive Psychologist, Elizabeth Loftus asked participants to recall being lost in a shopping centre as children. A quarter of participants gave explicit and vivid details despite never having been lost at all. They had produced the memory after Dr Loftus told them they had been lost, and their parents had confirmed it.

They believed they had got lost and so the story was formed.

The past is an illusion. Research in memory shows that 50% of what you recall from your past isn't true.

What if it didn't really happen the way you believe? What if it wasn't meant that way?

What if the thing that you are holding on to so tightly that is keeping you stuck in a past may not have even played out as you recall it?

Could you be anchoring yourself to a past that isn't even true?

Don't believe everything you think!

What are the story scripts that you need to start rewriting?

Next time you feel yourself getting lost in the story or interrupted by a negative thought I want you to imagine you are in front of a judge. You need to state your case about the story or belief but using only the hard evidence. Not what you think happened.

- *What is the truth and what is story?*
- *Ask yourself is this story or thought even true?*
- *What are you deleting, distorting or generalising?*
- *How is it serving you?*
- *What is the truth?*

Let's go back to the twins a moment, both had the same up bringing and experience, but they had a very different outcome, this is the perfect example of how it isn't the events but the response that shape us.

The way you respond when life is challenging will shape you. If you freak out or give up the minute something gets uncomfortable you will always find life a challenge.

Changing something as ingrained as your beliefs and stories can be like trying to walk down a very overgrown path in the woods, even without the added challenges of ADHD.

At first it is impossible to get down, the path is narrow and overgrown, so you have to make a real effort to get through.

Somedays, especially the days your state of mind isn't so good, you are tired, emotional or busy, you forget you have started using that new path and find yourself walking down the old familiar and worn path without thinking.

As time goes on the worn path becomes more open, it's clearer and easier to get through, you find yourself going down it without even thinking.

This is how coaching works, it uses the neuroplasticity of our brains to learn a new skills and ways of thinking. The brain is like playdoh, even ours, although the playdoh becomes harder to mould and easier to crack as we age which is why early diagnosis with a good after care plan is key for our future generations.

It isn't true what they say, you can teach old dogs new tricks. We just need to repeat them a few extra times to help them stick.

Our state of mind and the stories we are telling ourselves are the keys to deciding what paths we take, and they will override the most steadfast of strategies.

The *Square Peg* strategies you will learn in this book will help you create a brighter future, but they are useless if you are telling a shitty story or are in a bad state of mind, you will be forever going around in circles.

Letting go of your stories might require therapy, especially if there is trauma. This involves digging deep into your wounds which can be a painful experience. If you are struggling with ADHD symptoms it may be advisable to delay until you have stabilised the ADHD, so you are feeling more resilient, focused and positive before you lean into healing.

Think of your traumas and hurts as wounds, left untreated they can fester and grow poisonous. Cleaning them out is painful, uncomfortable and frightening. Remember your mum coming towards you with the TCP to go on your grazed knee, the fear of healing it was worse than the fear of living with it. But cleaning it out will heal it, leaving you with a strong, resilient scar filled with wisdom, rather than an open and vulnerable wound.

Tune In

What has resonated with you the most in this chapter?

Can you see where you your stories and beliefs may be holding you back?

Are you ready to start rewriting the script?

What is the new story?

What are your takeaways from this chapter and what can you put in place to help you now?

8

STRENGTH AND PASSION

'People with passion can change the world'

— STEVE JOBS

Passion and purpose are essential to the ADHD brain, if we aren't interested or inspired we probably won't be doing it for very long or it will feel like walking through treacle.

Square Pegs have ingenious minds, we are creative thinkers, amazing problem solvers and driven adventurers who see the world from a different perspective, as long as we are engaged and playing to our many strengths.

We like to be on the move, always growing and evolving. A *Square Peg* that values self-development, as you do is a powerhouse!

Growth is the key.

Finding your purpose in life can change your life. Some people, like myself are lucky, they have managed to combine their passion and purpose with their career, this is something I believe anyone can do, especially *Square Pegs* who were born to be Entrepreneurs!

An error people make is to mistake their passion for their goals. Your passion isn't the thing that pays the most or that gets you the best cars or the perfect body, passion is often something that has no material benefit at all.

Katie and I had been working together about eighteen months, it had been quite a journey and she had achieved some phenomenal goals along the way including getting a handle on her extremely stressful lifestyle, rebalancing her relationship with alcohol and turning her health around, losing three stone on the way. She was smashing through goals, gaining clients and even bought two extra houses with cash. She really was winning at life, or so it seemed.

One day she said to me, *"Kim, I thought it would be better than this."*

Despite everything she had achieved, something was missing. She had lost her purpose.

I knew what made Kate's heart sing because she spoke about it often. She loved cheering on her daughter's netball team at the weekends. Katie loved netball and had played at a high level in her teens. We talked about her getting more involved with the team and their training.

At first she was reluctant, she didn't have the time and it would just be too much. A month later she came on the call and told me she had stepped up to manage the team and was loving it. She was spending more time with her daughter, having lots of fun and feeling confident that she could move them up to the next league.

A year ago she wrote to me telling me she was still coaching the team and had started playing in a female league herself, she had found her passion.

If you are unsure of what lights you up then ask yourself these questions.

- *What would you do every day for free?*
- *What things do you do where time just disappears?*
- *What fills your heart and makes you feel alive?*

If you are feeling stuck with this, then it may well be that you have other things that are blocking you from knowing or following your passion right now, fear not, we are going to be talking about those blocks soon!

Celebrate and cultivate your strengths

Square Pegs can list their weaknesses easily, but ask them their strengths or talents and they stumble.

Years of constant effort and slog can knock your confidence and you may feel that you have no strengths and don't excel in anything. But we both know you do!

You have amazing talents, I have yet to meet a *Square Peg* who isn't extraordinarily good at something but I meet plenty who don't play to their strengths, or ignore their natural talents in favour of other things due to external pressures.

"I come from a family of lawyers, it was just what I was expected to do" a very unfulfilled client once told me, who thanks to leaning into her strengths and following her passion is now running a six figure pottery studio and selling her beautiful art as prints and cards via her social media audience.

Playing to your strengths means being in flow, and being in flow means feeling happy and calm.

Many of my clients have spent years focused on their weaknesses and trying to *fix* themselves so that they can fit in and make theirs and everyone else's lives easier. Focusing on trying to improve these areas is exhausting for our brains and only serves to exacerbate our ADHD challenges.

Remember, there are somethings that for your ADHD brain are a *can't*, not a *won't* or *can't be bothered*, but a simple *No*. Focusing on trying to improve these areas can leave you physically, mentally and emotionally exhausted frustrated and stuck!

Focusing on your *Yeses* and *Cans* will bring you much more success.

Rather than trying to make things that your brain struggles with happen, spending time and effort focusing on and improving your talents is where the success and magic lies. Confidence in your talents, strengths and ability gives you the motivation to create excellence in your life.

Happy and successful *Square Pegs* are those who focus on their strengths and outsource their weaknesses.

Your Physical and Character Strengths

Your physical strengths are the tasks, goals and activities you enjoy the most, usually the things you do most easily and are able to complete.

- *What are your natural talents?*
- *What do people ask you to help them with?*
- *What is something that you know you are better at than others?*

- *What do you know a lot about?*
- *Were there any subjects you enjoyed at school?*
- *Did you have any hobbies or interests out of school?*

Your character strengths are based more on how you think, feel and behave. They drive us and contribute to your personality.

Here are some that apply to *Square Pegs* especially…

- *Creative*
- *Driven*
- *Optimistic*
- *Resilient*
- *Kind*
- *Fun*
- *Knowledgeable*
- *Individualistic*
- *Persistent*
- *Tenacious*
- *Imaginative*
- *Passionate*
- *Inventive*
- *Enthusiastic*
- *Courageous*
- *Adaptable*
- *Versatile*

Which strengths apply to you?

If you can't see it for yourself, think how a friend, partner or colleague would describe you.

Are you creative, a big thinker, a problem solver, are you a performer, a singer an artist? Maybe you have talents that are sitting unused in the corners of your mind, if so, they might need some focus, maybe some up-leveling of skills or info.

Your strengths may need some work, some new knowledge or skills to really make them shine. If it interests and excites you everything else will follow!

Side Note Before you go off down an impulsive or expensive rabbit hole or hyper focused wild tangents, booking on courses or signing up to marathons....just take a pause!

I've lost count of the courses and programmes I've booked myself in on impulse in the past. Now I pause, give myself space and often phone a friend before making any big investments or life-changing plans.

Our impulsive ADHD and the phenomenal number of ideas we have can make it challenging to make the right decision at times, so I highly recommend having a friend, relative, peer or coach you can trust to run things by.

Many of us are verbal processors which means talking things through to get clarity really helps. If no one is around then speak it out loud to yourself, you can even record yourself so you can hear it back.

I'm a big verbal processor so am always speaking out load, running things by my partner, coach or friends. I've lost count of the times I have been caught having a full-on conversation with myself! #cringe.

Now my need to analyse events and situations in great detail before I can make peace and put them to bed makes perfect sense.

If you aren't much of a talker or sharer than that's fine too, just write it down or map it out before you dive in.

Tune In

What has resonated with you the most in this chapter?

What are your physical and character strengths?

How can you use the strengths more?

Do you need some extra knowledge or experience to hone these strengths?

What are your takeaways from this chapter, and what can you put in place to help you now?

9

RELATIONSHIPS AND FRIENDSHIPS

"Holding on to anger is like picking up a red-hot lump of coal to throw at someone; you will be the one who gets burnt"

— BUDDHA

B efore we start this chapter, I want to share a lesson from years of coaching hundreds and hundreds of humans.

People are good!

Even the ones who have hurt you and let you down.

Sometimes we make poor decisions and do bad things, often born out of hurt or fear and the desire to protect ourselves or our loved ones' reputation, ego or feelings.

Most people are doing their best, even though it might not be good enough.

No one wants to be a shitty person; really, they don't.

People often project what they are feeling, and I'm sure you have heard the saying *'hurt people hurt people.'*

Your Parents

I had a client who was able to make peace with her narcissistic, very likely undiagnosed ADHD, alcoholic mother because she came to terms with the fact that although her mother was lousy at the role of being a mum and her best fell short of providing her with the love and security she needed. It was her best; if she had the tools, she would have chosen to do better.

Many men and women have come to me over the years carrying a lifetime of hurt from their parents. We aren't born with instruction manuals, and so it is down to our parents to try and work it out with the tools they have.

Trauma is passed through generations until it is resolved; my client's alcoholic mother was very likely bought up through the eyes of her own mother's trauma. By working on herself, forgiving and moving on from her past, she can start breaking the chain of trauma for her future generations.

Intergenerational trauma is passed down via the stories we hear and the actions and beliefs of our carers. We are raised on their fears and expectations, this is how we turn in to our parents. Even though we may not like the traits we are displaying, they are automatic and driven by the beliefs our parents or main carer likely instilled in us when we were young.

Think of our histories, times of war, recession, pandemics and the constant power struggle of man.

My hero and a leading authority on this subject, Dr Gabor Mate, talked in an article about how this is even worse for us Brits due to our stiff upper lip mentality, Imperial past, boarding schools and the culture of *children should be seen and not heard*. He says we now see ourselves paying the price of suppressing years of emotion through the generations.

We are all born into trauma in one way or another, and of varying degrees, our best chance of peace is acceptance, self-awareness, self-development and moving on. All trauma can be hard to let go of, but childhood trauma can form as early as in utero and is embedded in us at the deepest level, creating our only reference and understanding of the world for the first years of life.

Trauma and ADHD

Firstly, let's have a look at a few facts...

We now know that ADHD is highly hereditary; you are five times more likely to have a father and twenty-four times more likely to have a mother with ADHD if you have ADHD yourself.

Until the 1990s, ADHD diagnosis wasn't that common, and ADHD wasn't believed to affect adults.

Women were and still are grossly under-diagnosed, especially the ADHD predominantly inattentive types.

Bearing all of the above in mind, if you carry a lot of hurt from your upbringing, could it be that you were raised by an undiagnosed ADHD parent who was doing their best?

I was an undiagnosed mum raising an undiagnosed daughter, and I can tell you, it was hell for both of us. I was that mum, trying to fit my beautiful, unique *Square Peg* into society's round holes, not because I didn't love her with every part of me, but because I wanted the best for her and to make her life easier, which at the time I thought meant fitting in.

I was very wrong, and it breaks my heart.

I didn't know any better, and I was doing my best at the time with every resource I had, as nearly every undiagnosed mother before me, including yours maybe?

Motherhood isn't easy, especially for women with ADHD who struggle to look after themselves. The added pressure of being responsible for nurturing other human beings and guiding them through life, so they are happy, healthy children is tough.

It's a huge responsibility, and no one ever gets it 100% right, ADHD or not. If we could change things, we would, but we can only go forward.

Fathers, siblings and other family members are doing their best with the tools they have too, which may also be limited due to their own issues and beliefs.

Close Relationships

Happy, harmonious, fulfilling relationships lift and open our hearts. They empower us and make us feel significant and heard. Ultimately they are the make or break of happiness. As social animals, we need each other and feed from the communities and company we keep who influence us greatly.

I have worked with several women whose closest relationships make them feel *crap* and have found themselves trapped in an unhappy union.

They stay because they believe leaving carries a heavy price tag, physically, emotionally and financially, especially in a marriage or partnership.

The guilt, inconvenience, pain, expense, time, and shame often keeps women in toxic, destructive, or unfulfilling relationships.

Some research and plenty of anecdotal evidence suggest that women with ADHD are vulnerable to ending up in toxic relationships, suffering physical and emotional abuse.

Developmental delays, low self-esteem, and the desire to be loved and accepted can leave them stuck in relationships where they suffer emotional abuse such as gaslighting, put-downs, rejection, fear, financial abuse, isolation and infidelity.

Finding the strength to leave these relationships can feel overwhelming to *ADHD*ers.

If leaving the relationship is the best solution, you don't have to do it right now; if you aren't ready. Remember your comfort zone, stretch it don't Road Runner it!

Acknowledging that things need to change, and you need to take action can be enough of a step to begin with. Get to work on yourself, start to build your strength and resilience so you can leave the relationship with a strong, firm and sturdy foundation of knowing who you are, what you want and what you stand for.

From this place, there is a better chance of an amicable split for all parties, including children.

The guilt over children often stops women from leaving difficult relationships. I have asked many clients who are living a miserable existence to keep their children happy what it is they are teaching them?

How are you teaching them to behave in years to come?

Are you teaching them that they are important and worthy? That they deserve to be respected, happy and free?

Or is the message to ignore their happiness and stay in an unhappy, violent or abusive relationship because of what they have, what people will think or because they were taught keeping the family together matters at all costs?

You can apply this logic to a host of situations, a bully boss, a toxic friendship, a vicious in-law, or an overly demanding job. Ask yourself what you would want your child to do in your situation, stand up for themselves and live the life they deserve or stay in a damaging situation hanging for dear life?

Women who stay in unhappy relationships or over-demanding situations have more health issues, hormonal symptoms, emotional dysregulation, and low energy; sadness is a heavy emotion.

Most people stay.

In reality, many of the clients I have worked with around their marriages stay. Working on yourself, cleaning out your closet, taking time for yourself and becoming your true self changes how you show up in life, and that changes most stagnant marriages or partnerships for the better.

Sarah came to me unhappy in her twenty-six-year marriage. It wasn't a bad marriage, she described her life as a good one, with happy children, money and health, but she and her spouse bickered a lot, often coming to loggerheads over chores or opinions. They didn't seem to share any interests outside of the kids, and he was always tired, so they never went out, which Sarah didn't mind as it meant she could squeeze in a few extra hours of work.

As we worked together, Sarah started to feel better about herself, and her energy was returning along with her confidence. She started to feel more in control of her day-to-day life and began looking after herself properly, eating well, working out and spending less time in the office and more time at home.

This all improved her sleep, gave her new energy and put a confident spring in her step. She had more balance in her life and found herself looking for less approval in all her relationships, especially with her husband.

As she changed, something in her relationship changed too. She was feeling less rushed, more confident and more alive. Dan noticed this change, even commenting on how great she was looking.

Instead of planning to leave, Sarah started working on breaking down some of the barriers she had built over the years. They talked about their resentments, especially around not having time for themselves in an ever-busier world. She opened up about her feelings on juggling work and the children, often feeling unsupported.

Dan said he understood, as he had felt exactly the same.

The truth was that under all those walls was the same love and friendship that had bought them together thirty years ago. As Sarah started feeling happier and showing up as her true self, becoming more open, vulnerable and less guarded, the relationship took on new energy, and Dan responded well.

Now when anyone comes to me telling me they want to leave a relationship, we work on them before we work on an exit plan.

Not all relationships make it through; not all deserve to. Some cannot cope with her in her full power, and others simply don't deserve to be there, but for those that are worthy, don't make the mistake Sarah nearly made, don't walk away without giving the relationship some attention.

How are you showing up in your relationship?

Does it need an overhaul?

Talking can sometimes be like pouring petrol on a fire. Doing is usually better. Can you organise to go out, for a walk, or for a meal? Try a change of scenery to see what happens when you let down some of the barriers and resentments that inevitably build up as we get busier with life and find ourselves having to make sacrifices to fit in with the needs of others. Especially when children and adulting are involved, it's tough...for all of us!

Friends, siblings and family

Relationships and friendships can be difficult for *Square Pegs*; developmental delays, sensitivities and extreme emotions can make navigating relationships and social situations difficult and confusing from an early age. Behaviours that come so naturally to neurotypicals can be a minefield for us.

Struggles with boundaries, emotional regulation, reading situations and others' emotions, environmental sensitivities, organisation, working memory, impulsivity, timekeeping, and just keeping up with others' lives as well as our own can make navigating friendships exhausting.

Many females with ADHD have difficulties fitting in with their peers from a young age, experiencing bullying or *'frienemy'* situations. The enormous sensitivity to rejection and instinctive desire to fit in can make these challenging times, leaving shattered self-esteem that filters into their adult relationships and friendships.

This can lead them to be over-givers, putting everyone else first and finding themselves constantly involved in others' dramas. Dramas feed our need for excitement, it's the same with people pleasing and helping out. Both increase dopamine, but both will also drain your batteries fast!

You don't always need to be saying *Yes* to everything, grabbing your hero's cape and saving the day. It is safe to protect your energy and say *No*.

This type of overgiving can often lead to exhaustion and resentment when our expectations of that person are not met. This is especially common if someone has a label like *mother, sister, best friend* or *spouse*.

We get hurt because we set our expectations based on how we believe the person with that label should behave. These expectations are based on our ideas, views and values, which probably aren't the same as theirs.

I used to be a big people pleaser; not everyone is, so when someone did or said something thoughtless or that I deemed to be selfish, I would feel hurt. What I have realised now is that my expectations of myself were often too low and the expectations of others too high.

Just because I dropped everything to help out or to fall into step with what someone else wanted, it doesn't mean they will or indeed should.

Realising this was a game changer in my relationships. Turns out, life is a lot easier if you just focus on keeping yourself happy first.

Who's in Your Squad?

The saying goes *"you are a reflection of the five people you spend most of your time with"*

- *Who do you spend most of your time with?*

- *List them out. Do these people lift you up? Do they fill your heart and make you feel alive?*
- *How do you behave around them? Do they bring out the best in you?*
- *How do they make you feel, about yourself, your life or your choices?*
- *What influence do those people have on you?*
- *Do they help you move forward?*

Managing your Relationships

Prioritising and understanding what's most important is challenging with ADHD.

Our lack of *Executive Functioning* and slow scrambled messaging systems means everything seems equally important to us. Hence, we can find ourselves carried away on a menial or unimportant task with no regard or urgency for the important stuff that needs doing first. Everything can feel equally important to us, making it easy to divert our time and attention to less important matters.

To help with this, I get my clients to create criterias for various areas of their life so they can take a pause and know what, or in the following case, who is important in an instant.

This first exercise can really help shift the dynamics of a relationship for the better! Giving you a criteria for the people allowed in your inner circle.

It works by scoring your relationships, which sounds a bit brutal. Still, just as we find prioritising tasks challenging, we can be the same with people, leaving us thinking everyone is equally worthy of our time, trust, attention and emotions, which they aren't.

This exercise can give you back more time and energy to spend on yourself and those who are truly worthy of it, plus it will save you feeling let down because your expectations were too high, or you have overshared or misplaced your trust in the wrong person.

When doing this, I want you to think of each person by their name, not their label. So Kim, Sally, Mark, Sarah. Rather than Mum, my sister, my husband etc., you get the idea, take the label away for a minute and see where everyone sits.

Just because someone has a label doesn't mean you have to spend time in their company if you feel crap in it.

If you have people in your life who repeatedly let you down, hurt you, or you feel self-aware, anxious, judged, or anything that means you have to try and fit into their round hole, then it is ok to step away in fact, it is more than ok, it is vital, no matter who that person is.

Your Relationships Criteria

First of all, you have your 10's - *Your 'Ride or Dies'*

These are the most special people in your life, they are in your inner circle. You can tell them your darkest secrets and deepest fears. No one gets to be a ten just because they have one of the labels loaded with expectations such as partner, parent, child, sibling, best friend etc.

They get to be a ten because you feel safe and happy in their company, you trust these people, and they can trust you.

These people let you be yourself and you them; no masks needed. You can be vulnerable, honest and open. It is important that these relationships work both ways.

Spending time with these people is a must; their company energises and brings the best out in you.

Then you have your 9's - *Your Besties.*

These are the best people that you love to spend time with. They can be lifelong friends, family, special colleagues, etc.

These people empower you. They are special people you can have open conversations with and bring value to each other's lives.

They know some of your secrets, you might not be quite as open with them as your 10s, but there is trust and respect.

These are the people or events that you make sacrifices for and let your hair down a bit. They are worth the hangover, the late night or the inconvenience. But it is still ok to say no to them. In fact, 9's and 10s are the people you can say no to without any fear, and they won't mind a bit; they will understand.

You will only have a handful of 9's and 10s in your life. If it is too crowded in your inner circles, it's easy to find yourself over-giving or over-sharing with the wrong people.

Next are the 7's and 8's - *Your Friends*

These are the people who are fun to hang out with, you have shared interests or hobbies, they make you smile and laugh, you feel good around them, and there is mutual trust and respect, but they are not the people you would have the deeper conversations with. They can be people from work, peers, a club or community.

They can also be family members or friends that used to be nine or ten, but things have changed, and it's time to move on and step back a bit.

There may be times in life when you have a strong common interest that brings you closer together, but in the main, these are people who you might be more reserved with and try to hold back from the oversharing that *ADHD*ers can find themselves doing.

You may feel like giving these people extra time and energy, and that is ok, but ensure you are giving it because you want to, not because you feel obliged to, and check your own time and energy bandwidth first.

Next are the 6's and 7's - *The Passing Throughs*

These are acquaintances, friends of friends or someone who is just passing through your life that you have formed a bond with. They are good people whose company you enjoy, but you don't spend much time with them or have close proximity, and you know they probably won't be around forever. They may be a neighbour, local mum or fellow gym member.

Then there are the 5'and 4's - *On the Perimeters.*

These people you may wish had a higher score but don't because the relationship makes you feel awful and brings the worst out in you. Maybe they have a label or something that means you can't push them out of your life completely, maybe an Ex you co-parent with or an In-Law you can't stand.

These people stay at arm's length, get the minimum amount of your time or bandwidth and are seen only when necessary. You need firm boundaries around these people to ensure there is civility on both sides.

Finally, the below a 4's - *Adios*

These are the people who don't belong in any of the categories above. It might be an old friendship that has changed or turned sour, but you still treat them as though they are higher up the hierarchy of your relationships, leaving you open to hurt and giving away your time and energy when really they need to go.

This doesn't mean burning bridges, far from it. You don't have to say a word to them, but from now on, things have changed.

You can still smile and greet them when you see them, have a quick chat or ask how they are, maybe send a birthday card *(which is a joke, because if you are anything like me, remembering birthdays and arranging cards is not one of your strengths!)* but then you excuse yourself and get on with your life, without them in it!

This isn't an easy exercise, but it really can be the change your key relationships need.

Emma's mum made her feel like crap; she was always putting her down, her children, her appearance, her home; nothing she did was right. Being together usually ended up in some argument. Each time was exhausting, leaving her feeling full of guilt and like a complete failure.

When we worked through this exercise, Emma burst into tears because she realised her mum was on the perimeters, and it broke her heart.

We put some boundaries around spending time with her mum and changed the dynamics of how they spent time together. Rather than having her round to the house, she suggested they meet for coffee or go on a walk which meant the meetings were less personal and that Emma was able to keep them shorter. She gave no explanation as to why or how things were changing, as that would have just caused another argument. Instead, she took action.

Over the next few months, with the extra self-development work Emma was doing, things started to improve with her mum. They started having better conversations and fewer arguments. Emma tells me now that her mum is actually one of her besties and that she feels fine that her mum isn't at the centre of her circle because now she understands that her mum is doing the best she can.

When I was interviewing women for this book, they told me how they had previously hyper-focused on relationships. Overgiving and over-sharing, which they now understood, could feel stifling and overbearing for their new friend. This high intensity had lost them friendships, causing them a lot of confusion and hurt at the time.

I did this exercise at one of my workshops, and at the end, a lady told me she suddenly realised she had been letting everyone in her inner circle and treating them as a 9 or 10s.

Her expectations of her 7's and 8's were too great; she was giving them so much of her time and energy that there was little left for herself or her inner circles. There were also some people it was time metaphorically to say goodbye to.

You don't have to put up with anyone who doesn't bring joy, happiness or love to your life. Maybe you used to be best friends, joined at the hip, ride or die, but things aren't the same now. It is ok to move on.

There are many ways to remove yourself from someone without having to give explanations or fall out. You can start saying *No*; you can just start holding your boundaries.

What if you don't have any 9's or 10's?

What if your partner isn't a 10?

Both of these have come up in the past. If this is you, don't beat yourself up. Use this journey to discover what changes you need to make, and start working on and building your relationships.

Can you forgive?

This is a subject I broach very slowly with hurt and angry clients because forgiveness isn't easy. It isn't something you do for others, and it's not about letting people off the hook. You don't even have to speak to the person or tell them you forgive them; it has nothing to do with them.

This is about you. Hate, hurt and anger are heavy emotions to carry, and the weight of them can be exhausting and draining.

Forgiveness will improve your health, self-esteem, mood, confidence and relationships. It is about moving away from a victim mindset to an empowered one where you can let go of resentment and find peace and freedom so that you feel lighter, calmer and happier, free from the exhaustion of carrying those negative emotions.

We only have a set time on this earth, don't waste it on people that make you feel crap; free yourself by letting it go. You may not find this easy, to begin with, but if you can let go, you can be free.

To be able to forgive, you need to acknowledge and give yourself the validation of how you feel. Think about the emotions you experienced and how this hurt has affected how those emotions show up in daily life.

Think also about the person, try to see things from their point of view, could there be another reason for their behaviour? Their unresolved traumas or misguided perspective of the world?

Maybe there was a misunderstanding? What part did you play? Could you have been at fault, too, in any way? If so, forgive yourself too!

If it seems too much, then forgive the small things first; start practicing compassion and forgiveness in your everyday life. It is a good way to live anyway!

If someone cuts you up in traffic, think of them with compassion. *Maybe they are racing to an important place, I hope they arrive safely.*

When your colleague triggers you, maybe they are having a bad day. *I hope they are ok.*

Bless and release when your partner grates on you.

Get used to brushing off angry, low, energy thoughts and feelings.

Is there anyone in your life you would like to forgive?

How would it be to be free of the emotions that person or situation stirs up?

Write down or talk your feelings out - whatever works best for you, especially if you are a verbal processor who needs to talk it out to get it clear; if you have no one you can talk to talk it out to yourself, I do it all the time these days!

Writing a letter can help.

It is up to you if you choose to send the letter or not, only you know if and when you are ready for that, but if you do decide to send a letter or have a conversation, be prepared for the fact that the person may not respond as you expect, be ready to let that go too. This is for you, not for them.

Forgiveness may need some therapy and the chance to work through it with a professional in a safe environment.

I know things I have talked about in this chapter may seem over simplistic in view of your situation, but if we are looking to heal from our past, we must lean in to clean the wound and learn to let go so that we can enjoy the here and now and allow ourselves to step a little further back from our stories.

Tune In

What has resonated with you the most in this chapter?

Where can you improve your relationships, and what or who needs to go?

Which relationships do you intend to give more time, love and fun to?

What are your takeaways from this chapter, and what can you put in place to help you now?

10

ADHD STRESS, BURNOUT AND KRYPTONITE

L ooking after ourselves is vital for *Square Pegs*. It's easy to get put on the back burner as we try to cram in, keep up and catch up with life. Bedtime gets pushed back, mornings get later, food gets faster, exercises get skipped, and time out irritates.

The women I work with usually live on the edge of burnout, slipping in and out of various stages.

Burnout featured heavily in my late thirties to mid forties until I was diagnosed at forty-eight. I would get so frustrated with myself, embarrassed to say how I felt when people asked, which most of the time was absolutely exhausted.

After burning out in my early forties, I learned to pull back and put my body before my business. It didn't mean that there weren't still days when I felt like I was walking through treacle or so on edge I could crack open and emotionally erupt like Krakatoa.

I'm still ADHD, and there were still plenty of times when I over-committed or overexcited myself and paid the price.

What I figured out long before my diagnosis and was absolute gold in helping me manage my energy was that I am a sprinter, I can step up and pull it out of the bag, and I can work with phenomenal focus and drive.

Before I learned how to manage my drive, it was a disaster that led to burnout every time.

I'd tell my husband *"just to warn you I am getting my head down"* to get whatever programme I was creating, launching or delivering done. It would mean late nights, weekends and early mornings.

Then like the proverbial Duracell bunny, the batteries would run out, and I would drop.

Without doubt, there would be some kind of emotional break-down, tears and tantrums, a complete lack of faith in myself, my abilities, skills, and confidence. There would be guilt at not doing enough or being around for my family - total meltdown, followed by withdrawal.

I remember the first time it happened.

I was thirty-eight, and the school holidays had just started, which are always a challenging time for any working mum. I had new venues opening up in my fitness business and new coaches that needed training; plus, to top it all off, we were going on a holiday with three other families that I needed to pack and prep for.

It was the first time I think I had experienced true anxiety, and I felt like I couldn't keep up with myself anymore. I was on edge the whole time, even when I was sleeping. I was used to being forever busy, but this was different.

I would get into bed at night exhausted and fall straight to sleep, only to wake up a short while later with my heart racing at 100 mph and a feeling of sheer panic.

It was always the same dream. I had something under my bed that I'd paid a lot of money for, and it had the answer on it. However, I wasn't using this thing; I had forgotten it and let it go to waste.

It would take me several awful minutes of deep breathing to finally calm myself down and get back to sleep.

Over the following months, this got worse until, in the end, I was waking up with a start that made my husband jump out of his skin, saying *"I've got it, I've got it"* and jumping out of bed to look under it for the 'thing", one time I came around in my son's room looking under his bed!

My husband would be going, *"What is it Kim, what's the thing?"*

I would wake up with everything racing. It was bonkers; in the end, I was scared to go to bed.

During the day, I would take myself off with the dog and purposely get myself lost in the woods. I constantly felt like I wanted to cry, but I was too scared to start because I knew I wouldn't be able to stop.

I was so busy, there was so much to do and organise, I was completely overwhelmed, and I knew I was in trouble. My husband would tell me I needed to go for a run, but that wasn't working anymore; in fact, it was making me worse and was the last thing I needed to do.

One day he came home from work to find me cleaning out the cupboard under the sink, which was his first red flag ...house-work was not my thing, and I NEVER did it, but in my head, it was really urgent, and it needed doing immediately! Right now!

I was talking at 100mph about everything I had to do for the holi-day, how everyone else was ready and prepared but I had nothing done, all whilst pulling everything out of this stupid bloody cupboard.

"Kim, stop," my husband said

"I can't. Don't make me stop."

He took my hand and said you need to go and lie down

"No, no, don't make me do that, please," I knew what was going to happen if I stopped

He led me upstairs, where I laid on the bed and burst into tears. I cried for what seemed like forever, and then I slept. That was on a Friday night. I didn't move and barely spoke for the rest of the weekend - the perfect example of the emotional flooding we talked about earlier.

On Monday, I finished the packing he had started over the weekend, and we went off on what was one of my favourite holidays ever. It was the first time I could remember that I hadn't taken some kind of work or study away with me.

It took me the best part of a month to even open my laptop after that, not because I was trying to be good, but because when I did, there was nothing there. I had sprinted for way too long, and my batteries were well and truly flat.

I was unaware of the damage I was causing from stretching myself for way too long. I thought I was invincible, I'm not, and neither are you!

Feeling stressed out, overwhelmed and under pressure has become the norm in modern society. Busyness has become another accolade of importance and heroism. We too often berate ourselves for not being able to fit it all in and hold it together like our peers who seem to be crushing it.

Side note Most are not; almost two decades of coaching has taught me no one has their shit together all the time. Scratch the surface, and you will see things are very rarely as they seem, so comparing yourself to these women is a fantasy. Give yourself a break because they don't exist!

When a high-achieving woman who appears to have it all together comes to me, I look for one of two things: regular down-times and a history of self-development or anxiety. I usually find the latter and work towards the former.

Stress is part of life and *Square Pegs* would be bored without it. It isn't all bad; there is the good stuff too!

When I had my next big burnout (I won't bore you with the story, suffice to say, same overdoing it, different day!), most of what got me there was great stuff.

I moved house, married the father of our children on my Fortieth birthday, went on several holidays and had a fantastic year in my business, all great stuff. I still put that down as the best year of my life, but stressful all the same. Without the right strategies, rituals and boundaries, I was soon retreading water.

When the waters got choppy and the big waves came, *my amazing mum, who is still with us and fitting fit, got a second breast cancer diagnosis, followed shortly after by a close friend's sudden death.* I once again started to drown.

Does it really matter?

The body constantly works to maintain homeostasis, which means balancing the many intricate systems that keep us running. It doesn't differentiate between good and bad stress; it just recognises that the balance is tipping and that the body is under stress, even if it's good.

Stress itself isn't the issue; it is our perception of the situation and the importance we place on the outcome that causes the stress, especially when we don't feel as though we have any power to control the situation or its results.

I am not saying that none of it matters, but I guarantee you a lot of it doesn't. It's just our thinking that makes it so.

I always get my clients to ask themselves five questions to help with perspective when they are in the middle of a crisis.

- *Will this matter in five years?*
- *Will it matter in five months?*
- *Five weeks?*
- *Five days?*
- *Are we going to survive this?*

Remember our *Square Peg* tendency to overthink, analyse and ruminate. This, coupled with our negative bias means we are always looking out for danger and the worst-case scenarios. Sprinkle in the executive functioning issues that make it hard to prioritise what's true and important, and you see why even life's simple challenges can seem overly stressful.

Being able to pause and give ourselves the space to work out what really matters and what is just noise is vital to our success.

Stress is a vital biological reaction to a potentially dangerous situation and is one of our basic safety mechanisms. During these times, the body will prioritise the production of the stress hormones Cortisol and Adrenaline over everything else. It needs to prioritise your survival. It has no idea if you are running late for an appointment, running off a Dominos or running from a lion, the response is the same.

Physically our hearts beat faster, and the blood rushes to the muscles, ready for mobilisation. Adrenaline is produced, followed by cortisol. When we are in this state of high alert, the body prioritises things like muscle strength so it can react fast and slows down the things we don't traditionally need in a *fight or flight* situation, like digestion, reproduction, and libido.

Mentally, the Amygdala (our fear centre) hijacks the prefrontal cortex (thinking / problem-solving centre), and all sense goes out of the window as your brain goes into red alert and steps up for survival.

Stress will make you hyper-focused on the perceived danger and lock out everything else, often including the solution.

Chronic stress eventually causes an imbalance in the body.

Here are some signs that your body might struggle to keep up with your fly-by-the-seat of your pants brain.

Check out the list below and give yourself a point for each thing you come across on a regular basis...

- *Poor sleep patterns*
- *Tension, backache and neckache*
- *Palpitations*
- *Restlessness and fidgeting*
- *Dry mouth*
- *Shakiness*
- *Exhaustion*
- *Sweaty, clammy, flushed, tense*
- *Stomach upsets, indigestion, ulcers*
- *Thyroid problems*

- *Allergic responses such as itching, rashes and asthma*
- *A tendency to gain fat around the middle*
- *An increased appetite*
- *Increased cravings for a combination of carbs and fats*
- *Mid-afternoon slump - needing a coffee and snack to get going*
- *Low immune system - catching every bug going with a slow recovery*
- *Blood sugar swings*
- *Digestive problems – bloating, flatulence, diarrhoea*
- *Muscle Aches and Pains, especially neck/ shoulders*
- *Hair loss*
- *Difficulty concentrating/ forgetfulness*
- *Depression*
- *Irregular/ absent periods*
- *Increased PMS*
- *Decreased / absent libido*
- *Tiredness but can't sleep well - known as tired but wired*
- *Getting a second wind later in the evening*
- *Waking up during the night and can't get back to sleep and then over sleeping in the morning*

How did you do? Where is stress showing up in your body?

There are certain things that are like Kryptonite to ADHD brains, and stress is one of the biggest.

Stress will exacerbate our symptoms; pouring petrol on what might only be burning embers under normal circumstances.

Your ADHD traits will show up in technicolour.

Your impulsivity will rise, and your hyperactivity will increase, showing up physically with the need to move either by fidgeting, interrupting, over-talking, over-sharing, overdoing, over-giving or cognitively with racing, catastrophising thoughts that take over your entire day and leave your stress response chronically switched on so your body is working ten to the dozen to deal with the continuous excess of cortisol.

You will drop more balls, make wrong decisions, have more emotional floods, and quickly take your stress levels to the limit.

Stress affects your immune system, stopping it from responding as rapidly as it needs to. Cortisol is an anti-inflammatory that stops you from getting ill and enables fast healing after injury. But chronic elevations and repeated burnouts can lead to the immune system becoming resistant to its effects. Pushing your inflammation levels high, making you susceptible to illness and slow recovery.

I have repeatedly seen this in clients frantically treading water and getting cold after cold until an infection or virus causes total wipe-out, followed by months of exhaustion as the adrenals slowly recover.

This is why stress is so damaging for us, left untamed it can cause diseases that can be fatal.

Think of it like *the boy who cried wolf*. If we keep telling the immune system that there is a wolf every time we are late for an appointment, our bodies won't be able to tell the difference between that and real stress.

I could go on, but you get the point, stress sucks, and *Square Pegs* tend to suffer more often and more intensely.

The good news is there is a solution to stress management that doesn't involve shutting down your whole life and living on a hippy commune, although some days that does appeal to me! Or maybe you have those days where you say, *"this is too much; I just want to jack it all in and get a normal 9-5."*

You don't and you won't, you aren't wired that way, you have ambition and drive, you wouldn't last five minutes, but it's a phrase I hear from my high-flying clients on a regular basis, and I use myself at times.

Perception

If we learn to understand and shift our thoughts, we can begin to work on changing our perceptions of the events in our life. Remember, it's not those events that shape us but the way we react to them. The one thing we can control (with a bit of practice) is our perception of, and reaction to them.

Our bodies are constantly tuning in to our thoughts and interpretations of what is happening around us, always ready to pick up and react to any stress you might be feeling.

If we can get to grips with our perception of stress, we can change how we deal with it physically, mentally and emotionally.

How we view stress matters.

In a study on the perception of stress and its effect on mortality, 30,000 Americans were asked two questions:

How much stress have you experienced in the last year?

Do you believe it is harmful to your health?

Then they checked public health records for the next eight years to see who died.

The bad news was that people who said they experienced a lot of stress in the last year had a 43% increased risk of dying, BUT that was only true for those who believed it was harmful to their health. If you didn't believe the stress was harmful, you were in the group with the lowest risk of dying.

Researchers estimated that over the eight years they were tracking deaths, 182,000 Americans died prematurely, not from stress but from the belief that stress is bad for you.

I bet every single one of those participants had stress in their lives. It's the perfect example of why our reaction to the stresses, traumas and events in our lives is so important. If we get perspective on the situation, we can lower our physiological response to it, saving our lives and sanity.

Besides that, cognitively, we can think straight, stay better focused and start finding solutions!

Sidenote *If you are stressed because you're forever overloading your plate, you need to take some stuff off of it. Start to look at where the triggers are in your life.*

Maybe you feel all the positive thinking isn't going to change a situation. If that is the case and you have things you need to work out, heal or get off your chest, then working with a coach can help. Maybe even a therapist if you have a lot of healing to do. Because life is too short as it is, racing through it at 100 miles an hour is no way to spend it, ADHD or not.

Do you create stress in your life for the buzz?

*ADHD*ers don't do boredom; our brains crave stimulation and arousal, even if it's unhealthy for us. This can lead to addictions to food, alcohol, drugs, sex, spending, scrolling and drama.

Stressful situations, arguments, and drama create an adrenaline rush that becomes its own reward for our excitement hungry brains.

Looking back, I can see how I would seek out these dramatic situations and dramas in my younger days.

I once had a boyfriend who, despite being a nice guy, was pretty messed up. He was a *bad boy* who was often in trouble and came with a lot of drama. We would fight badly all the time with disastrous and dangerous consequences.

Although this was so unhealthy for me and caused me a lot of pain and hurt, I was completely addicted to the relationship. When I finally managed to leave, I struggled for a long time without the nervous energy that the constant danger of life on the edge gave me. Normal relationships seemed boring, and I would often just drop a little hand grenade into proceedings to liven things up.

It wasn't conscious, and I had no idea what I was doing or why, but hindsight is a wonderful thing. Looking back, I can see many areas of my life where I would pull the pin and chuck a grenade in to liven things up, even when the outcomes were dangerous or to my detriment.

Do you find yourself chucking grenades in every now and then, especially when things are going well or calm?

Picking fights, doing destructive things, taking reckless chances?

Psychologically there can be many reasons for this, but neurologically for an unstimulated ADHD brain. It's often just another way to liven things up a bit.

High-risk dangerous activities like fast driving or extreme sports increase dopamine and motivate our brains; this is the reason why *ADHD*ers make great emergency service workers; they perform at their best and love the thrill of the intense pressure.

When there is not enough drama of their own many *Square Pegs* can find themselves bang in the middle of other's dramas, stimulating their brains with intensity and excitement.

Ever been called a *drama queen*? If so, then don't panic; now you know, and by the end of this book, you will have a list of other ways to hit that high without pulling the pin!

Where do you spend most of your time?

Stress can be good in the right way; it can focus our energy and sharpen our senses, getting us motivated and cooking on gas, but you have to know how to ride the wave!

There are four main zones.

The Comfort Zone

This is our rest and recovery zone, it's a nice place to be, but it isn't very stimulating and can quickly get boring for us *Square Pegs*.

Think of how you feel when you go on holiday, it's nice, *once you finally relax*, but after a while you look forward to coming home and getting on!

Maybe you can't help yourself thinking of work?

I love being on holiday it is great for my business; I can come up with so many new ideas when my brain and body are idle.

The comfort zone is vital for creativity, perspective and recovery, but it isn't somewhere you want to be all the time.

There is no growth in the comfort zone, which means it can get boring, there is no excitement, which is dangerous for us.

The Stretch Zone

This is your on-fire zone, where the balance is perfect, and you are at optimum stress levels. Your energy is high; you feel focused, productive and get things done. Your ADHD powers shine through!

This zone isn't without stress, but stresses are seen as challenges, chances to level up and grow. Being in this zone makes you feel alive.

However, regularly stepping back into your comfort zone to rest and recover is vital. We can feel so invincible in this zone that we become over-excited and over-commit, filling our diaries, taking on too much and pushing us into the strain zone.

The Strain Zone

We all must go into the strain zone and pull it out of the bag sometimes. Everyone has times you need to get your head down and get on with it until the event has passed or resolved.

It can be the lead up to a happy event such as Christmas, a holiday, special birthday, moving house or a wedding.

An important deadline, or big project to pull off at work. Or one of life's curve balls such as divorce, redundancy, or family illness.

We can survive in this zone without doing too much damage for short periods, especially if we are in there with a positive growth mindset that can help us rise to the challenge. But you can't stay there.

You have to be like a ninja, in and out.

If you spend too long in the strain zone, the stress overload will eventually become too great, and you will see your symptoms ramp up and take over. Leaving you feeling fatigued, short-tempered, anxious, overwhelmed and ultimately ineffective.

Some people spend so long in the strain zone that it becomes the new normal. They get so used to feeling rushed, overwhelmed and exhausted, that they don't realise they are running into trouble.

I see a lot of clients who have spent too long in this place, and it's where I used to live too!

Getting out of the strain zone after having spent years living in it can feel like a struggle, especially for hyperactive *ADHD*ers who use a lot of their excess energy up in this zone.

Spending time in the comfort and stretch zone can feel uncomfortable. Their mind and body are so used to being in a heightened state they can find themselves self-sabotaging their calmer lives to get back to feeling *'normal'*, even if that normal is a racing mind and exhausted body.

I had a client recently who said, *"Kim, I feel like I am going backwards with my stress management. My levels are rising again, I'm finding myself back in the strain zone most of the week, and I don't feel good at all"* when we got on a call and drilled down to what the stresses were she discovered they weren't really that stressful at all. She just wasn't used to dealing with issues and not feeling stressed, so was perceiving everything as a big stress that called for time in the strain zone.

A shift of perception allowed her to hold her boundaries around her time and get back to her comfort zone for some R&R, ready to step into her stretch zone and shine.

As you shift your mindset and make changes to your lifestyle, you will start to feel more at ease resting, connecting and recharging in the comfort zone, finding more activities that give you the high of the strain zone without taking you out of the stretch zone such as exercise, fun, and laughter.

Failure to master life out of the strain zone will lead you to the next zone.

The Panic Zone

This is where things are really starting to fall apart. Your physical and mental health will start to suffer, your ADHD will be through the roof, and you are at risk of serious life-changing implications.

Life in the panic zone sucks and can take years to recover. If you feel like you are in the panic zone right now, this is your warning and permission to use this book, take the steps you need, and get yourself out fast!

Tune In

What has resonated with you the most in this chapter?

How is stress showing up in your body?

What zone are you spending most of your time in?

What are your takeaways from this chapter, and what can you put in place to help you now?

11

NATURAL HIGHS – EXERCISE

When I first started understanding what having ADHD meant and that I had it, there was one question I kept asking myself.

'Why haven't I had as many issues as others? How have I got this far?'

One answer was genetics, ADHD is a spectrum and I was not as *ADHD* as some and more *ADHD* than others.

But the other reason was there was one thing I had done consistently since my early thirties. I had looked after my health.

I exercised and ate well, adding meditation and prioritising my sleep to the list early in my forties.

These four pillars have become as much a part of my life as my ADHD, without a doubt they have kept me on the straight and narrow …ish!

You can't self-care ADHD into submission, there is no known diet, supplement or strategy that is said to cure ADHD, but there are plenty of natural things we can do to manage our symptoms.

Movement

If there is one thing that helps our brains focus, it's movement. fifteen-twenty minutes of heart-raising activity will give you two to three hours of focus!

Exercising increases our dopamine and norepinephrine and, when done regularly, encourages the growth of new brain receptors and improves the structure of our highly malleable brains.

Along with improvements to the blood vessels and increased blood flow, helping us think, plan and control our emotions better, exercise increases activity in the prefrontal cortex, positively affecting behaviour and attention whilst releasing the endorphins that make us feel good.

It also improves the efficacy of ADHD meds for those on them.

Complex exercise that involves balance and coordination, such as racket sports, rock climbing, gymnastics, martial arts and yoga, are great for ADHD as they combine the mind and the body, thus challenging the brain simultaneously.

Although the best exercise for ADHD is the one you find interesting, challenging and enjoyable, whatever that might be, because, without those winning elements, the chances are you won't stick to it.

Choose things you find fun, dancing, hiking, swimming, anything that gets your heart pumping and your body moving.

My exercise of choice is strength training, and it is one I am passionate about getting all women involved in. Lifting weights makes women feel strong in their minds and bodies.

Square Peg Exercise Strategies

Ignite interest and inspiration by finding something you like to do, play a sport or join a club.

Starting your day with exercise helps with the structure and routine we need, avoids procrastination and ensures you are optimally alert to start your day.

Exercising in a group setting can increase motivation and adherence.

Use split timer Apps like Gymboss to keep you focused and on track. Setting the timer for 40/20 so you do 40 seconds, work 20 seconds rest for 20 rounds will give you 20 minutes of exercise.

Make it easy by having clothing, trainers, equipment, and gym bag ready to go the night before or already in the car.

Create a habit by making it regular and have set days and times so it is easier to remember and stick to. Make an appointment in your diary.

Add interest and excitement with rewards and celebrations.

Use the power of positivity. Remember this is part of your mission to be a better version of yourself, big yourself up and celebrate every milestone, goal or achievement you smash along the way.

Focus on the outcome rather than that process. Most people don't like exercise, myself included at times, but I love the feeling and high afterwards that is always worth the effort.

Next time you procrastinate, ask yourself where your focus is and who's running the show, you or your ADHD?

The hardest part of any workout is getting your trainers on.

Make a deal with your brain that you will do three minutes, and then you can stop if you want.

You can turn back home, put the weights down, leave the class - I use this strategy for running all the time, and it never lets me down!

Tune In

What has resonated with you the most in this chapter?

What active pursuits do you enjoy?

How can you add more exercise to your day?

What do you need to put in place to make regular exercise easier to adhere to?

What are your takeaways from this chapter, and what can you put in place to help you now?

12

NATURAL HIGHS – NUTRITION

F ood can be a big and complex challenge for *Square Pegs*. One of the most common impulses female *ADHD*ers struggle with is eating.

The other is spending!

Impulsivity makes us more prone to eating when we are not hungry and less able to regulate our choices and calorie intake.

Choosing sugary, high-fat dopamine-inducing foods, mindlessly and automatically picking, especially when bored or unstimulated.

Square Pegs often carry a lot of shame around food. Many have battled with weight gain most of their lives, seeing it as another example of their inability to pull themselves together.

Studies show that obesity, bulimia, and binge eating are more prevalent in those with ADHD due to impulsivity and lack of control.

Understanding that someone with ADHD is four times more likely to be overweight and that our behaviour around food isn't greediness, but the brain's craving for dopamine and an inability to control its impulsivity is a relief to overweight women I work with.

It has also been shown that candidates for gastric bypass surgery, with a body mass index above the 90th percentile have a very high rate of undiagnosed ADHD.

Lack of executive functions makes doing what we say we will do and sticking with our health goals, hard work. Planning meals, keeping the fridge stocked with healthy options, rustling up a nutritious dinner and fitting in a workout can be much tougher for us.

I have never had an eating disorder, but my eating is very disordered.

I am an impulsive eater, often eating as I prepare food to such an extent that I sometimes have no appetite for the meal.

How about you?

What sort of eater are you?

ProcrastinEater

Is when snacking meets procrastinating and is my downfall. I dread to think of the excess calories consumed whilst writing this book! Snacking can help overcome the anxiety of a looming deadline giving the brain that much-craved hit of dopamine and relief from the mounting pressure.

Impulsive Eater

You have an impulsive, uncontrollable need to eat constantly - grazing throughout the day, especially in unengaging environments or trying to complete tedious tasks. This can be due to the lack of stimulation rather than being greedy.

Feast or Famine Eater

You go most of the day without eating as you are hyperfocused until you suddenly feel emotional, shaky or on edge as your blood sugars drop, and you grab the quickest, most convenient, energy-dense food to you, like yesterday's leftover pizza, or a biscuit.

Hoover Eater

You eat fast, barely letting your food touch the sides, without tasting or savouring the flavours. You can eat a lot of food in a small amount of time and often have second and third helpings as you don't give yourself time to feel full.

Sensitive Eater

You stick with a narrow range of foods, usually ones you liked as a child, where you were probably labelled a fussy eater. Your strong sensitivity to texture and taste can mean certain foods taste revolting, making even trying them traumatic.

ADHD food kryptonite

I am not about to lecture intelligent women like you on the dangers of too much sugar, processed foods, E numbers, trans fats, alcohol or caffeine in the diet. You know that, but I can't finish this section without sharing the foods that cause inflammation in the body and disrupt hormones exacerbating ADHD symptoms.

I have coached health and wellness since my early thirties, and there is one thing I have learned: the further we move from nature, the fatter and sicker we become.

Whilst I have tried different strategies and methods with clients over the years depending on their issues and circumstances, my founding principles have always been the same, no matter what the current fashion or trend, natural is always best. Mother Nature has our back.

We need to fill our plates with lifeforce foods and avoid the CRAP.

Caffeine

Refined Sugars

Alcohol

Processed foods

We will feel healthier, happier and more able to manage day-to-day stresses, energy, and ADHD symptoms.

Our bodies are made of billions and billions of cells, and every cell reflects the health of your body as a whole.

They need a constant supply of high-quality macronutrients from carbohydrates, fats and proteins and micronutrients from vitamins and minerals. Fail to supply these, and you are starving your brains and body of nutrition.

Many of our foods these days are stripped of their nutrition by modern food processing methods, and so much of today's food is full of chemicals and additives that our bodies cannot process and do not know what to do with.

ADHD may not be caused by these chemicals or poor nutrition, but it worsens it.

Here are four foods I recommend you consider eliminating or limiting from your diet for optimal energy, health, easier management of ADHD symptoms and losing a few pounds if you want to.

Sugar and processed foods

Sugar is more kryptonite for *ADHD*ers, especially children. Dopamine-deficient ADHD brains are wired to look for highs and kicks. We are predisposed to crave sugar due to the surge of dopamine it delivers to the brain.

A Swedish study recently found that *ADHD*ers were twice as likely to have Type two diabetes.

Sugar, refined carbs and processed foods mean energy-dense high-calorie foods with no nutritional value that burn energy fast. Elevating blood sugar levels and insulin, increasing the risk of type two diabetes and ramping up ADHD symptoms.

These foods upset the mineral balance in the body, causing hormone imbalances, depression, fluid retention, high blood pressure and heart disease, which puts us on a hormonal roller-coaster and in a perpetual cycle of hunger, tiredness, irritability, sickness and weight gain.

Sugar also breaks down the immune system, preventing it from defending the body from invading forces. Did you know that an average white blood cell can destroy up to eighteen different bacteria before it's killed? However, by the time there are twenty-four teaspoons of sugar in the bloodstream, that number drops down to one!

If you consider that a fizzy drink contains an average of eight to ten teaspoons and a Mars bar contains over seven teaspoons, you can see the pressure the immune system will be under from just one poorly chosen snack.

The western diet is full of sugar. It's hidden all over the place in meat products, bread, sauces, fruit juices, breakfast cereals, and even healthy ones! As well as in the usual places like cakes, sweets, fizzy drinks and biscuits.

This quiet infiltration makes sticking to the World Health Organisations six teaspoons a day maximum a challenge unless you are eating freshly prepared non processed food.

1 teaspoon = 4 grams.

How much sugar is in your diet?

Wheat and Gluten

Gluten causes inflammation, bloating and poor digestion in a high percentage of the population, resulting in intestinal and digestive problems leading to weight gain, unbalanced hormones, Celiac and IBS.

It can leave you tired and heavy and is where people usually feel the most significant change after eliminating it from their diet, as the stomach feels less bloated and energy levels increase.

There is no objective evidence that eliminating gluten and wheat from the diet improves ADHD unless the person has a gluten intolerance, autoimmune or Celiac disease, but that isn't why I have included it. I have included it because of the mountain of other scientific nutritional evidence and my anecdotal findings from coaching women who have felt so much better after getting it out of their diets.

Why not try taking it out of your diet for a week and feel the benefits yourself?

Caffeine

Can give us a fast dopamine boost and a quick energy surge that can improve attention and focus. Bingo! Just what we need, right?

Not really. No, I like to get my clients to use caffeine as a tool.

Not everyone metabolises caffeine well; some people can have adverse side effects like anxiety, sleep issues, racing heart, headaches, migraines, muscle tremors and jitters from just a small amount. Those who can handle it may have similar effects from overconsumption.

Like so many things with ADHD, some people feel better on it, some worse, but those who overuse caffeine can end up with the adverse side effects listed above.

If you are a slow starter in the morning, then a cup to get you up and going, with maybe another mid-morning can be good.

My kettle never used to get cold, I was constantly topping up to keep myself focused and going, but after struggling with my sleep, I use caffeine more strategically these days. I go days and weeks without it, but if I know I have something I need to focus on, I will have a cup of tea and use the benefits it brings.

I have advised clients who don't use it regularly to have a cup before a big meeting or presentation to give them a boost in focus and concentration.

I have also used it as a boost when struggling with energy.

If you can metabolise caffeine, then this works.

- *Drink a caffeinated drink of your choice.*
- *Set an alarm for 15-20 minutes, maximum - I use my phone.*
- *Put it out of reach – I put mine on the other side of my office.*
- *Lay on the floor and close your eyes - I don't make it too comfortable. I just lay flat on the floor.*
- *Meditate or sleep.*
- *When the alarm goes off, get straight up and turn it off.*
- *Give yourself a minute to come round, then 54321, leap into action.*
- *Don't go over 20 minutes as you will fall into the deeper stages of sleep where it is harder to wake up, leaving you* feeling groggy.

Do this for fifteen to twenty minutes max, and no snoozing allowed!

Sidenote Caffeine isn't just coffee, it's in normal tea, green tea, hot chocolate, colas, and energy drinks. The more caffeine you drink, the more you need. It is an addictive cycle.

Caffeine can cause more side effects when used with ADHD meds, although many report not needing so much caffeine once they start medication.

Alcohol and ADHD

I am no teetotaler and enjoy a beer at the weekends, so I am not about to tell you to stop, but alcohol is like pouring petrol on ADHD.

I changed my tempestuous relationship with alcohol back in my early forties after the sudden death of a close friend floored me, and I realised that alcohol was making the grieving process harder and even more unbearable.

My weekend binge drinking left me feeling anxious, depressed and overly emotional, taking me until at least Wednesday to recover, giving me a day of feeling level-headed before I was back down at the pub Friday.

I had no idea how I'd do it, as it meant pulling back from my social circle and friends for a while, but like so many of the women I work with, I surprised myself, and it wasn't as tricky as I had thought it would be.

It is well established that men, women and youngsters with ADHD are more vulnerable to developing an addiction than their peers. *ADHD*ers are twice as likely to abuse or become dependent on alcohol or cocaine and 1.5 times more likely to develop a cannabis addiction.

Self-medicating with drugs or alcohol isn't uncommon in women with ADHD, who often begin experimenting at a young age, and earlier than their peers.

I have worked with lots of women who struggle with alcohol, leading to much misery, shame and regret.

As with food, if your relationship with alcohol is unhealthy, out of balance and causing problems in your life, then ADHD can make reducing or abstaining difficult, though by no means impossible.

As with everything we have spoken about in this book, whilst your dopamine-deprived, thrill-seeking ADHD brain isn't your fault, it is your responsibility, and there are things you can do to change this relationship.

Clients who successfully changed their relationship with alcohol started by making changes in the areas of their lives that caused them the most stress and made them want the drink in the first place. Once they feel happier, more aligned the alcohol is less of a tool to change their state of mind, helping them forget whatever is making them feel stressed, depressed or unhappy and more of an occasion at social events.

There's a whole identity attached to alcohol, like a relationship that you know is toxic, but you don't see how you would cope without it. Women have told me they fear rejection if they don't drink, saying alcohol gives them confidence, helping them fit in.

They use it to cope with a tough day or celebrate a good day and panic about how they will deal with life and their feelings if they don't drink.

When my clients tell me they have had or want a drink, I answer the same as I do for food.

It's not having the drink that's the issue. It's about who you are when you pick up the drink. Are you enjoying a lovely moment with a friend, or are you desperate to get that first glass down you to feel better?

Alcohol is a poison to our bodies. That feeling when you are woosy, giggly and talking jibberish, is caused because you are intoxicated, i.e. *poisoned*. Over the years, your body adapts, meaning you can handle higher levels, or so you think.

Is your relationship with alcohol something that is causing you problems or needs looking at?

Sidenote ADHD medication, along with an appropriate support programme and plan, has been proven to help many addicts or bingers overcome their need to self-medicate with all forms of addiction. Don't be afraid to try medication if you feel like your impulsive or addictive behaviour is becoming a problem. However, you do need to be officially diagnosed to get access to medication.

Square Peg Nutrition Strategies

Timed eating - try to overcome impulsive eating with a regular eating schedule. If you can, have set eating times for meals and snacks throughout your day.

You might try ...

8am Breakfast

10.30am Snack

1pm Lunch

4pm Snack

7pm Dinner

8pm Small Snack

Use plates - avoid eating directly from packets and out of the fridge.

Hide food away and put it out of sight so that you aren't constantly subliminally triggered and reminded.

Don't diet - aim for a healthy eating plan rather than one with restrictions. *ADHD*ers aren't good at being told they can't do something, so give yourself some slack and allow treats and occasions where you can. Otherwise, you will risk hitting what I call the *F it button* and going wild in the cupboards!

Start your day with protein to kick start the brain's neurotransmitters and make sure that every meal and snack is protein-based using food such as meat, fish, eggs, tofu, beans and legumes.

Eat plenty of good fats such as olive oil, avocados, nuts, seeds and oily fish such as salmon, mackerel, sardines, trout and herring to fill you up for longer, feed your brain and balance your hormones.

Choose complex carbohydrates such as sweet potato, squashes, rice and quinoa or higher protein carb choices such as legumes, beans and grains if your gut can tolerate them. Keep your carb consumption low if you are trying to lose weight, avoid carb-based snacks and choose at least one carb-free meal a day. With your evening meal, a small portion of starchy carbs like those above can help induce restful sleep.

Eat a lot of veggies, and aim to eat all different varieties throughout the week, with leafy green veg playing a strong role!

Non-starchy vegetables should cover at least half of your plate with a serving of protein, some good fats and a small number of starchy carbs.

Fruits are nature's sweets. They make a great alternative if you have a sweet tooth, but eat smaller amounts of the lower sugar fruits like berries if you want to lose a bit of weight.

Include Omega 3 fatty acids; numerous studies have shown the benefits of Omega 3's for reducing ADHD symptoms. It's the supplement with the most substantial research for cognitive function, with one study showing a 50% improvement in symptoms.

Choose either a good quality supplement with equal doses of EPA and DHA or include three to five portions of oily fish such as salmon, mackerel, sardines, trout or herring in your diet each week.

ADHD symptoms have been linked to a deficiency in the vitamins Zinc, Magnesium, Vitamin B and Vitamin D, all of which are found in a balanced diet. If you feel you are not getting enough, you can add supplements, but food is always a preferable source.

Drink filtered water throughout the day to help keep hunger at bay.

Have a two-drink limit, most people can have two small drinks and feel mildly tipsy but still able to make decisions and stay focused. That third drink is often the one that tips things over the edge. It might be different for you, especially if you are on medication. For you, one might be enough and two is over the edge, be honest with yourself and set yourself a limit.

I know it's obvious, but it does work like a charm... drive!

Driving can trigger that fear of missing out or being perceived as boring, but give it a whirl and try a night out without drinking, you'll be surprised at how enjoyable sober can be.

Stick to single measures and avoid cocktails or shots.

Remove the temptation to drink during the week by removing alcohol from your home.

Tune In

What has resonated with you the most in this chapter?

What changes can you make to improve your nutrition?

What needs to happen to make these changes easier to implement?

What are your takeaways from this chapter, and what can you put in place to help you now?

13

NATURAL HIGHS - SLEEP

S leep is our primary source of rest and recovery, any disruption or lack thereof will have a big impact on mood, energy, hormones, general health and ADHD symptoms.

Sleep disturbance makes emotional regulation and clear-thinking tough, increasing Amygdala activation and causing the brain to ruminate, creating repetitive, negative thinking and more of the emotional flooding that we are prone to.

Scientists have even proven a link between sleep and procrastination. They discovered that one night of sleep deprivation negatively impacts our ability to transition from task to task.

Sidenote They also say naps can benefit task switching, so if you are stuck, take a quick nap and return to it.

Ultimately, if you don't sleep well, regularly or deeply enough, you are physically and psychologically under-recovered and under-repaired, creating numerous side effects that make getting on top of ADHD virtually impossible.

Just look how a five-year-old behaves without sleep - they simply cannot function, we are no different!

Sleep can be problematic for *Square Pegs*, as physical and mental restlessness can disturb our sleep patterns.

Struggles with shutting down our minds at night can mean difficulty falling asleep; hyperactivity can cause light and fitful sleep, as well as *Restless Leg Syndrome*, which is higher in the ADHD population. When we do wake up in the middle of the night, our fast brains and racing thoughts kick in, making getting back to sleep tough.

Many *ADHD*ers find themselves awake until the early hours of the morning when they finally fall into a deep sleep just hours before the alarm goes, making waking up difficult and over sleeping a regular occurrence.

We find sleep boring, a waste of our precious time when there is so much to do, particularly if we haven't used enough physical or cognitive energy throughout the day. Many women, especially mums, find they can think clearly and feel more focused late at night when the house is quiet, and disturbances are minimal.

One client told me how she would stay up as late as possible, pushing herself to get the most out of the day and trying to get everything on her never-ending to-do list done, beating herself up for not having achieved enough during the day.

I used to do it myself, especially when the kids were young. I was always first up and last to bed, just to try and fit my endless list of tasks in. It wasn't unusual for me to be up till two in the morning, ticking off all the tasks I'd struggled to stay focused on during the day.

I convinced myself I was a night owl and most productive at night. I would get to the evenings feeling exhausted, desperate to close my eyes, and then at 9 pm, I would suddenly get a burst of energy, crack open my laptop and proceed with my working day.

I wasn't a night owl, but I was turning myself into one by disrupting my circadian rhythm and cortisol output, meaning my mornings were a foggy mix of snooze buttons, caffeine and running late, finally feeling awake by about 10am.

The Circadian Rhythm

Our circadian rhythm is governed by light and the 24-hour body clock that controls sleep and wake cycles. Most living organisms have one; it is the reason flowers close at night and open in the morning or that birds all sing at daybreak and flock home at dusk.

It's this rhythm that controls the sleep hormones Cortisol and Melatonin. Think of our hormonal cascade like an orchestra. As one hormone rises, another one drops, and all should be in perfect sync.

In the case of sleep, our cortisol levels should start to rise in the early hours of the morning, just before dawn, preparing you to slowly wake up, peaking around 9am, making you feel alert and raring to go, then slowly declining throughout the day hitting a low around 8-9pm when the pineal gland will start to produce melatonin, and you will begin to feel sleepy.

Melatonin continues rising until it peaks around 3am, then slowly declines as cortisol rises, and you begin to wake up around daybreak, a beautiful dance and one that can give you a great start and the chance to get ahead of the day.

However, modern-day living and artificial light, especially blue light, interferes with this delicate cascade sending misleading messages to our already dysregulated brain.

When this rhythm gets disturbed, our cortisol starts kicking in at night, just as we should be winding down, hence that burst of energy we can get later in the evening despite having dragged ourselves through the day.

Blue Light

This is the light emitted from the backlit displays on screens, such as, your phone, tablet, laptop etc. Smartphones emit the highest levels of blue light compared to other devices, and because we hold them so close to our faces, the exposure is maximised.

Blue light hits further back in the eye than any other light, but the cells they hit have no relationship with the eye and are instead a direct connection to the brain. These rays tell the body it is daytime even if it's midnight, disrupting the circadian rhythm and affecting melatonin and cortisol production, screwing up our sleep patterns.

It is linked to sleep disruption, anxiety, depression, racing heart (I wake up with this about 30-60 minutes into sleep if I use devices late at night), increased alertness and the reduction of REM sleep when we dream, which means less problem solving and *emotional filing*.

Like all light, blue light should follow night and day. Technology has broken that rule, and we are now exposed to it 24/7. We naturally get energising blue light from the sun, which is why getting straight out into sunlight is great for waking you up in the mornings and has been used in the treatment of SAD Syndrome, it isn't, however, so great just before you're going to bed!

If you struggle with sleep, the good news is many of my clients have managed to reset their body clocks and improve their sleep by following the strategies below, it might take a few weeks to really embed, but many clients see results just by getting off their phones before bed.

Lying awake at night

There is nothing worse than lying awake at night with your mind racing. This is especially common in ADHD inattentive types who suffer from cognitive hyperactivity. If you find yourself lying awake ruminating in the dead of night, here are some techniques to help you try and get back to sleep.

Start with the truth, is what you're thinking about really true or is your busy, bored brain just making stuff up.

Practise 4-7-8 breathing

Calm your fears with the mantra

"I am safe, and everything is as it should be", or we/he/she/they are safe.

Keep a journal by your bed so you can write it all out.

If you regularly wake up in the night with stuff on your mind, writing a to-do list before you hit the hay can signal to your brain that nothing will be forgotten, and will be dealt with after a full night's sleep.

Tell yourself you cannot solve this problem now and promise you will revisit it in the morning when you are able to take action and resolve it.

The biggest thing is not to worry about waking up.

We all naturally wake up several times throughout the night as we move between sleep cycles, we just don't remember it. If you find yourself waking up, tell yourself it is just the natural rhythm, and you will be back asleep in a minute.

Often what happens is we wake up and start to panic and worry about getting back to sleep, and how that means we will be tired the next day, what if we don't wake up on time etc, before we know it, we have fired up our brain and away we go, when really waking up in the night is normal.

Other strategies include:

- *Listening to sleep stories*
- *Sleep meditations*
- *Yoga Nidra*
- *Tapping or EFT - Emotional Freedom Technique*
- *Reading*

Square Peg Sleep Strategies

A good night's sleep starts in the day.

Aim to get up at the same time each day, even at weekends, as this will help reset your body's clock; erratic sleep/wake schedules can disrupt the body's circadian rhythm.

If you struggle to wake up easily, get out in the daylight immediately. Maybe have your morning cuppa in the garden, an early walk to start the day or just put your head out the window. The light will encourage your body to produce the cortisol that gives you your get up and go.

Take ADHD meds early in the day, so they are out of your systems by the evening.

Have a small snack before bed to help blood sugars stay balanced throughout the night.

Aim to get thirty minutes of daily exercise, but avoid exercising after 7pm, especially cardiovascular exercise that will increase your cortisol levels and leave you buzzing.

Avoid caffeine after 12pm - caffeine has a half-life of six to seven hours, meaning if you have your last coffee at midday, half of the caffeine from that dose will still be in your system at 6-7pm; it also has a quarter life of twelve hours, which means a quarter of that coffee's caffeine will still be in your system at 12am.

Sleep expert Dr Matthew Walker says it is the equivalent of drinking a quarter cup of Starbucks just as you hop into bed and expecting a good night's sleep.

Stay away from activities that arouse you or get you hyper-focused late in the day so you can start unwinding before bed.

Most mothers know that the more routine there is around bedtime, the easier their children settle, we are the same. Good sleep hygiene and a calming bedtime routine are vital to getting those ZZZs in if you are struggling to sleep well.

A warm Epsom salts bath in the evening can really help. When you get out, just wrap yourself in a towel and lay on the bed, allowing yourself to dry naturally so your body absorbs all the magnesium that will relax your muscles and aid sleep.

Supplement with Magnesium Glycinate or Malate 200-400gms or Magnesium spray an hour before bed. Magnesium supplementation can also help ease restless leg syndrome, something ADHDers can suffer from at night. Iron supplements are also believed to help with this.

Get off your gadgets by 9pm. Yeah, I know, it sounds tough - at least get off your phone by 9pm and use a laptop instead (if you have to), but my gold standard is off gadgets by 9pm. This gives your body's melatonin the perfect environment to do its work. It also means the chance to shut the world out and have some time without social media, celebrity BS, shopping or whatever it is you are spending time scrolling or swiping through. Take a break from all the comparisons and other negative emotions these activities can bring up.

Aim to get to bed early; 10pm is ideal, but no later than 11pm.

Keep TVs and gadgets out of the bedroom, keep this room for sex, reading and sleeping.

Practise 4-10 rounds of the 4-7-8 breathing technique below before sleep.

Breath in for 4, hold for 7 and out for 8, making the noise of the sea.

If you forget, just think in for 4, out for more!

Breathing this way helps calm the nervous system and quieten the mind.

Tune In

What has resonated with you the most in this chapter?

What changes can you make to improve your sleep?

What does your evening routine need to look like?

What are your takeaways from this chapter, and what can you put in place to help you now?

14

NATURAL HIGHS - MINDFULNESS AND MEDITATION

Training your brain to slow down long enough so it can pause, even for a second, is one of the most powerful strategies for managing our super-fast brains.

Meditation and mindfulness will help slow down your thoughts, so you can see when a thought is just a thought and let it pass. You will be able to make better, less impulsive decisions that significantly affect your actions, giving you improved results and a calmer, more balanced life.

Mindfulness and meditation reduces negative rumination and helps you regulate your emotions and reactions. How we feel is important because how we feel determines how we act and the choices we make, which in turn impact our results and outcomes.

Regular practise thickens and strengthens our prefrontal cortex, the home of executive functioning, building new connections, and increasing focus, whilst improving concentration and the ability to do what you say you are going to do.

I know that meditation with a brain like ours can seem challenging. The idea of sitting still in silence can shut our brains down before we even get started. When I mention meditation to clients, I see them visibly recoil.

My brain won't shut down

Let me tell you a secret, no-ones brain shuts down, it's not meant to. That would be like your heart stopping beating.

This calmer way of being was a journey for me, it took me a long time to go from talking about it to actually putting it into practice, but once I started, I was hooked! I now meditate most mornings and practise mindfulness throughout my day; it's a great tool to calm down an overactive or negative mind bringing you into the safety of the moment.

The easiest way of doing this is to appreciate and notice the things close to you, a simple flower or view, a stranger's smile, anything, just notice what's around you.

The other way is to go into and notice yourself, how you are feeling, taking your focus to your feet, your bottom on the chair or your heart beating.

Noticing your breath is always a good place to start.

You can do it anywhere - walking the dog, queueing at the supermarket, sitting in the car waiting for a child, you don't even need to close your eyes.

- *Focus on your breathing,*
- *Feel your hands on a surface.*
- *Your feet on the earth*

- *The feeling as you relax your shoulders*
- *Release the tension from your jaw.*

Focusing only on that particular moment, not judging or criticising, just noticing and observing. It's so simple but so effective! Think of it as a chance to shut down all the tabs you have open in your head, just like you would reset a hanging computer.

I meditate first thing in the morning, usually sitting up in bed, to reduce the chance of any distractions like unloading the dishwasher, opening my laptop or, the biggest mistake of all, checking my socials.

I use a free version of an App called *Insight Timer*; there are several really good free guided meditations of various lengths that help with all things, including productivity, focus, calm, confidence, anxiety etc.

For me, I just set the timer and breath in through my nose and out through my mouth for fifteen minutes or so. What I love about this timer, though, is that it allows you to set chimes at intervals throughout, which can help keep you on track.

I'd start with a short session and set the chime for every minute when you first start, so you have a reminder to bring your wandering mind back to the breath, mantra or moment.

Finding your mantra

Sometimes I use a mantra. For example, I'll breathe in, thinking *Calm Mind* and out thinking *Happy Heart*.

I started using this when I felt my meditation wasn't working as well. I was getting easily distracted again, which makes sense.

Meditation is like anything for our brains; you have to keep mixing it up otherwise, it will tune out!

Another mantra I suggest to clients when they are feeling over-whelmed or anxious is *I am safe, everything is as it should be* it's a great one for the middle of the night when the mind can tie you up in knots or when you are in a situation where you have no idea of the outcome, and the only thing you can do is trust that the universe, your god or fate will look after you.

Other mantras you can use are:

- *Calm/Peace - When I feel on edge, this always brings me back*
- *Om*
- *Abundance/Gratitude*
- *Joy/Love*
- *Breathe/Still*
- *I am strong, I am healed*
- *I am important/ I am worthy*
- *Follow my heart*
- *Everything is as it should be*
- *One step at a time*
- *This is me*

Anything that sits with you goes, there are no rules; just don't try and force it. If you don't want to do anything guided, you don't fancy the breathing, and you don't resonate with any of the mantras above, then try this.

Close your eyes, put your hand on your heart, take a few deep breaths to still the mind and ask, *What do I most need to hear right now? What do I want to feel?* Let your inner self-guide you to the right words for you.

If you are just starting out, I recommend putting three minutes on a timer and practising the *Calm Mind, Happy Heart* mantra first thing in the morning, although I have had clients who do it on their commute and mediate on a crowded train.

That really is the beauty of mindfulness and meditation, once you know how to do it, it is a tool you can use to calm your thoughts and your nervous system at any time with no one needing to know. It helps you understand and see your thoughts as simple occurrences in your mind, passing like clouds rather than something that needs a reaction.

Not every meditation or practice will go perfectly. In fact, you will find some days that your mind is bouncing all over the place, and that's ok. Meditation isn't about perfection, it's about practise and training the mind to focus on the moment and be calm.

Think of it like a workout. Some days are amazing, others are just ok, but you keep doing them because you know it is doing you good! It's the same with meditation.

Gratitude

We have learnt that to ensure our survival, the brain preferentially scans and stores our negative experiences over the positive, making human beings inherently negatively biased, acting like Teflon for the good stuff and Velcro for the bad.

Now add the 50-70,000 repetitive and often negative subconscious thoughts we have a day, and we can see that a lot of unwelcome negativity is holding us back and not serving us at all well.

Consciously focusing on the good stuff daily at every opportunity is the antidote that will increase your positivity bias and wellbeing. A daily gratitude practice is super easy, fun and a great way to train your brain to shift focus from the negative to the positive.

The art of gratitude is backed by science.

Gratitude and positivity can shrink the Amygdala, helping us stay more positive from day to day and moment to moment.

When we appreciate the very small things in our lives, it helps move our attention to everything that's right and teaches us to spend more time focusing on the good things and less turning the slightly negative into a *'Woe is me'* vortex of doom.

Thanks to our highly palpable playdoh-like brains, when we repeatedly practise gratitude, eventually we become more wired to look for the positive in daily life, making even the most negative of situations a challenge to be overcome rather than a disaster to finish us off.

Bookending the day with gratitude

Each morning give thanks for three things in your life.

There are two rules:

1. You can't pick the big ones, but you can pick some of the smaller things about the big ones, like a cuddle from my son or a great chat with my daughter, my garden, the lovely lady I get my morning coffee from, finding a tenner in an old coat pocket, it can be anything.
2. You can't pick the same thing each day.

I have had clients who have found this impossible at first. If that's you, start with three things you are grateful for within your family, kids, pets, partner, friends, parents, or three things you love about where you live or three people you are grateful to have in your life.

If you are really struggling to start, keep it simple:

- *I ate today.*
- *I have a bed to sleep in.*
- *I drink clean water,*
- *I have nice clothes.*
- *I am breathing.*
- *Someone cares for me.*
- *I have my freedom.*

Then, before you go to sleep, ask yourself three great things that happened today. I get my clients with young children to do this as a game before bed, and I love it because it fires up their positivity bias in a way that will serve them for life!

When I have clients who are struggling with self-esteem or confidence, we make the gratitude more personal.

Three great things I did today.

- *Gave a great workshop.*
- *Kept my boundaries strong with my boss.*
- *Spoke up in a meeting.*

Three things I love about my body

- *That it is strong enough to move the living room furniture (possibly for the 3rd time that week if your hyperactive brain is on one!)*
- *That my hearing is so good, I can still sit at the back and not miss a thing.*

- *That my skin is so soft.*

Three ways I made a difference today.

- *By mentoring a young colleague at work.*
- *Sharing something I read in this book with a fellow female who is struggling.*
- *Called my mum to check in on how she was doing.*

If three is too many, start with one, and if you are still stuck, think what a friend would say if they were reviewing the way you showed up that day.

The important thing is that you take some time out to celebrate the beauty of life and your personal wins and successes every day.

Square Pegs are not great a being their own cheerleaders. They are so used to focusing on the areas in life where they struggle or feel they failed (nearly always down to undiagnosed ADHD) that they are often stuck for words when talking about their own accomplishments and strengths.

Especially if you are the mum, the boss, or you work alone.

How often have you got a standing ovation or even a pat on the back because there is food on the table, clean underwear for everyone, and you've managed to coach your struggling teen on a friendship issue? Not very often, I bet!

So, from now on, I am tasking you with being your own cheer-leader and never letting a success or achievement pass by without shaking your pom poms.

Tune In

What has resonated with you the most in this chapter?

How can you start your meditation journey?

What prompts can you use around you to take a mindful moment or give gratitude during the day?

What are your takeaways from this chapter, and what can you put in place to help you now?

15

THE SQUARE PEGS TOOLKIT

I t all sounds great doesn't it?

I hope you are feeling fired up with ideas and plans on how you can turn your life around and make this all happen.

However, if you are anything like I used to be, you will have a fantastic week, feel phenomenal, bursting with inspiration and plans, then life will get in the way, and things will be back to normal in no time, leaving this book gathering dust beside the bed.

Newsflash, you are not going to change anything by wishing for it. You are going to need to work for it consistently!

It isn't going to be easy. I'd love to tell you different because there are people in this world for who this sort of thing is easy, but if you have a neurodiverse brain, that's probably not you.

Easiest for you will be sticking to what you have always done and how you have always done it.

But then guess what happens? You will get what you have always got and everything will stay the same.

Change is hard, but Hal Elrod's words help spur me on.

"First it's unbearable,

Next, it's uncomfortable,

Then you're unstoppable."

What's in your ADHD toolbox?

Your toolbox is your list of *daily dos* and *must-haves*. These are the things that make you feel and act better. They help you think, focus, decide, stay on time, get going, feel happy and give your brain the fuel it needs to be the creative, fast-thinking, fun-loving, solution-focused, ingenious super brain it is.

It's best if you make your own list with what works for you but here are some ideas if you get stuck.

To help me focus at work:

- *Timer*
- *Brown Noise*
- *Fidgets*
- *Clock or watch*
- *Notebook*
- *Phone out of sight*

To help me feel my best:

- *Meditation*

- *Healthy diet - you can be more specific here. Mine would be fresh foods whilst staying wheat and sugar-free.*
- *Exercise - again, be specific. Mine would be strength training*
- *Gratitude*
- *Walking*
- *Baths*
- *Bed by 10.30pm*

What's in your first aid kit?

These are your *fast-acting go-tos* if you find yourself on the brink of burnout; again, you know what works for you in times like this. Think of the places you go and things you do to recharge your batteries. Keeping your toolbox well stocked should mean you experience less and less of these edge-of-your-seat times.

Here are a few ideas if you're stuck

- *Perspective*
- *Sleep*
- *Time out*
- *Time alone*
- *Exercise*
- *Friends or family time*
- *Fun - what do you love doing? Mine would be walking, wild swimming or eating out.*

Create motivating habits

When we let unmotivating habits sneak in (lying in, a daily glass of wine, buying a chocolate bar in the petrol station), we feel unmotivated!

Make things easier with action-triggering habits and routines. This way, you protect your goals from distractions, bad habits, or energy and motivation zapping internal shall I, shan't I, dialogue.

For example:

> *"I work out straight after my first coffee"* triggers the action that once your coffee is finished, it's time for your workout, rather than *"I'll work out tomorrow."*

When I boil the kettle (habit 1), *I meditate* (tagged on habit).

As my dinner is cooking (habit 1), *I make something healthy for tomorrow's lunch* (tagged on habit).

What habits can you tag on and automate?

Think of things you already do to which you can tag something else.

Procrastination

So now you know what's in your toolbox. All you have to do is use it!

Of course, there will be times when you can't seem to get going, but the key to success is to expect things to be hard and plan how you will overcome them. The time and effort we use procrastinating, wishing, berating, and guessing is much harder than just getting on and doing it.

Always remember, the hardest part is getting started.

Next time you procrastinate, ask yourself where your focus is and who's running the show, you or your ADHD?

Make a deal with your brain, do three minutes, and then you can stop.

You can turn back home. You can put the weights down. You can get a takeaway instead. But I bet you don't!

Getting going is the hardest part.

Once you have momentum, it's easy to keep going, you might even enjoy it! Just don't let the thoughts hold you back, GET OUT OF YOUR WAY!

Are you focusing on the process or the outcome?

Never focus on the process unless it's something you love doing. If it is unengaging, inconvenient, or you can't seem to transition to the task, then the outcome is where you need to focus. Think about the end feeling, and start towards the thing immediately.

Just take the first steps. They are the hardest. Remember the 3-minute rule, you can stop after three minutes if you want.

Successful people focus on the outcome rather than that process. Try this, rather than:

- *Getting sweaty and uncomfortable during a workout.*
- *Standing cooking.*
- *Having a tough conversation*

Focus on:

- *The buzz and focus after a workout or a decent night's sleep.*
- *Confidence in your jeans.*
- *Freedom from a toxic situation.*

Go for the low-hanging fruit

If the task seems too overwhelming, the untamed ADHD brain will shut it down, leaving it frozen or stuck which means it doesn't take action, leaving us feeling like a failure.

My clients with big goals, start small and celebrate every win and achievement along the way. It's the success and feeling you are on the right track that gives you the motivation to keep going. The longer you keep going, the more successful and motivated you become.

Clients use it a lot with exercise motivation.

If you want to start running, for example, don't do a 5k on day one. Start with a run around the block, then repeat it at set times three times a week. It only needs to be five to ten minutes long to start.

The important thing is to create the habit, and the rest will follow.

Ask yourself what small changes you could make to reach your goal.

If it is to save money start taking lunch to work or making some other small but significant cutback and put the saved money in a savings pot within your bank account. As your savings grow, you will feel more motivated to make other cutbacks.

Side Note I bank with Starling. I moved from my bank after 42 years because it was so archaic. Money management has never been one of my strengths. Unless you want it spent fast, then I'm your girl! I love Starling. It's much better for my Square Peg brain.

You can see what you spend and where, and set up savings pots within your account that you can round your spending up. It's great to watch it grow.

I have one pot called money not spent, and every time I go to buy something, I ask myself if I'd rather have the money in my bank. Usually, nowadays, it's the bank

PEG - Pause - Evaluate - Galvanise

I have talked a lot about pausing, and hopefully, you are starting to use it already. Doing the work outlined in this book will help you do it more often and easily, but pausing is only half the process.

Our *Square Peg* brains don't have the best sat nav systems; they aren't great at planning routes for us, so we need to train ourselves to stop and look at the map now and then so we don't get sent off course by our faulty signals.

The PEG process is super simple to remember and designed to help you prioritise what is most important before you head off following another shiny object. Like everything in this book, the more you practise it, the more your brain will recall it for use when needed.

Pause

This is your prompt to become aware. Stop and observe how you are feeling and who is driving your brain right now, You or your ADHD.

It's a chance to check in with how you feel; the body is a master at feeding back feelings to you; those feelings are the connection to your intuition and internal guide.

Taking that all-important moment gives you the chance to move on to the next part of the process.

Evaluate

We have learned that we are easily distracted and that our brains are wired for interest, not importance, so we need to check what we are focusing on and if it is part of the plan.

Ask yourself these questions.

- *Am I doing this because it is important or just interesting?*
- *Is it in the plan?*
- *What are the priorities?*
- *What is most important?*
- *What is the least?*
- *What can be deleted?*
- *What can be delegated?*
- *What is the next step?*

Galvanise

Now we have to make it interesting and ensure we have everything in place to get the plan started and keep it happening until the end because, if we get bored or distracted, things tend to either not get finished or drag on for ages. *How long's that bag for the charity shop been in your boot?*

Ask yourself these questions.

- *How can I make or keep this interesting?*
- *How will doing this help me or someone I love?*
- *What is the prize? What is my reward, tangible or otherwise, for getting it done?*
- *What is the ideal environment or circumstances for me to do this task?*
- *What do I need to help me focus?*

How does this look in real life?

It's Monday morning, you wake up and immediately feel over-whelmed.

Your head is bursting with things you need to do, and your brain is telling you everything is urgent, so every time you get started on a task, the next task pops in your head, distracting you and diverting your attention to that task, leaving the other one half started. Then an email pings up, and you feel the instant need to respond to that. Before you know where you are, it's lunchtime. You've been busy all morning but have achieved nothing and still have all the important tasks to do.

And then you remember to PEG it - Pause, Evaluate, Galvanise.

You answer the questions and realise you have been doing the day-to-day tasks that are easy to tick off and get a dopamine hit with. The quick feel good wins rather than the priorities.

You work through the questions, list what you need to do, decide to outsource a few bits, and work out your next step.

You remind yourself that getting your accounts done is going to help you feel calmer and mean you could relax tonight knowing they were done.

You put on a favourite tune to fire your brain and energy up whilst you get your environment right and find a quiet clear workspace, maybe not your usual seat place or position. (I work all over my house to keep me from getting bored) load up some brown noise on YouTube to help you concentrate, put your phone on silent and out of the room or at least completely out of sight and away you go, everything set for success.

Tune In

What has resonated with you the most in this chapter?

How can you make using your Toolbox daily easy?

Where can you use PEG to keep you moving forward in your daily life?

What are your takeaways from this chapter, and what can you put in place to help you now?

16

BEFORE YOU GO...

F inding rituals, strategies, habits, hobbies, people, places, and careers, that support you in all of your technicolour *Square Peg* glory is the key to living in harmony with your ADHD.

I hope that this book has given you the strength, courage and tools to go and live the life of peace, calm and happiness you deserve.

I want to share with you the traits the coolest *Square Pegs* I know have in common.

- *They are the happiest and best version of themselves TODAY, living in the moment as much as possible.*
- *They don't compare themselves to others.*
- *They listen to their intuition and value their judgement.*
- *They understand that they are responsible for their happiness, and they can design the life they want.*
- *They see that all challenges are chances to learn and opportunities for improvement.*

- *They have clear and active boundaries that they uphold.*
- *They don't take responsibility for others' emotions.*
- *They invest time and energy into their self-care*
- *They don't stay stuck in old hurts.*
- *They aren't scared of change.*
- *They are brave and always open to moving forward.*
- *They value their importance.*
- *They have strong values that they use as their internal compass.*

Moving On

If designing the life you deserve means making significant changes to key areas, I wish you the very best on your journey and want to tell you that I categorically know you have the strength to do it. I know you have the strength to keep going when it's tough, no matter how tough it gets, because I have worked with women like you who've done it with great success!

If there is a better life for you, then you need to use the strategies in this book to keep that end goal at the top of your mind. I have coached women through difficult and heartbreaking separations from partners, family, businesses, friends, and careers, but once the dust has settled and they feel in full flow with life, they know it was worth every tricky step of the way.

I know you can do this!

If living your happiest life means just working on a few key areas, then now is your chance. Maybe your relationships need some love and attention, your environment needs a good sort out, or you need to forgive someone, the same applies.

Keep things that are important in your life close by, family and friends included. Have usual visual reminders, that you move around from time to time, so they don't just blend into the background, as things do when our brains get used to them being there.

Either way, whether they are big or small changes, focus on what you CAN do and what you CAN control, rather than what you can't and if you feel stuck ask yourself what small step you can take to move forward.

Then make a plan.

For example, maybe you think, *"I hate my job, but I can't be without the money."* This may be true, but you can start to look for another job and make plans to move on.

ADHD doesn't just go away

Even medication doesn't work alone. You need to find, learn and implement the strategies that work for you. This book won't make a blind bit of difference to your symptoms unless you take some action.

(Congratulations for getting to the end of the book, by the way! Finishing a non-fiction book before starting another is something I have to consciously focus on these days!)

Before you put this book down, I want you to list what you will take away from it. What tools you are going to use, and how you are going to put them in place.

Then if you want to ace it, write the tools that help you most and how you will apply them down daily to help you stay focused.

My biggest hope is that if you didn't already, you now know you are not alone. I see you and want you to shine.

Misdirected symptoms of ADHD can be embarrassing and feel shameful, leading to negative thoughts or behaviours. *Square Pegs* are masters of stuffing it all down and slapping on a smile. *No woman wants to be the one who can't keep her crap together.*

But now you know. Now you know it is more challenging for you than the neurotypicals in your life and that if you feel like you are failing, it is most probably because you are aiming higher and already working harder than everyone else.

You wouldn't believe the high-flying women I speak with who tell me they aren't doing enough, yet they are doing ten times more with their lives than most people I know.

Cut yourself some slack. You've been doing life with one hand tied behind your back. Only you would get more patience, understanding and help if you did have a hand tied behind your back so everyone could see.

People would try to help you in noisy, crowded places, give you extra time to get ready or out of the door and give you a hug instead of a look when you snapped because things were just so hard.

They would accept there were things you couldn't do and try to make life easier.

Only people can't see, and until now, you may have felt very alone in this neurotypical world where you never entirely fitted in.

I hope now you feel ready to dance to the beat of your own drum and be proud to wear your ADHD badge.

Because we are different, not better or worse, just different and we weren't born to fit in!

What do you love about your brain?

I want to leave you with some of the comments I have collected from women about their brains as part of my research for this book.

- *I love that I am creative and drawn to help others.*
- *I am an amazing problem solver, and I love learning.*
- *I notice things.*
- *I'm creative and can come up with some weird and wonderful ideas, plus I can hyper-focus when something is interesting.*
- *It allows me fun and freedom and not be stuck in a dead end 9-5.*
- *The incredible ideas I have.*
- *I love that I am creative, curious and compassionate.*
- *I love that my brain constantly wants to learn and can switch quickly between tasks.*
- *Caring, empathetic, logical, organised and able to see far deeper than others.*
- *I love my ability to multitask and get things done quickly when I am hyper focused.*
- *I love that not many things get me down.*
- *I love that due to my forgetful memory. Even when I'm upset, angry or frustrated, I soon forget what I was even upset, angry or frustrated about.*
- *I love its brilliance.*
- *I am confident in achieving exceptional projects that few others would undertake.*
- *I love how others respond to and are attracted to my confidence.*
- *I love that I have unique ideas and can develop them.*

At the end of each interview, I asked the question.

"Would you change your brain?"

Every woman said exactly the same thing.

"No way, but I wish I'd known sooner."

I couldn't agree more.

But now we know!

It's time to do this, ladies!

Are you ready?

ABOUT THE AUTHOR
KIM RAINE

Kim is a straight-talking, High-Performance, ADHD, Mindset and Health Coach.

Having spent over 17 years coaching health and mindset, ADHD found Kim in 2019 when a client was diagnosed. It turned everything she believed about ADHD on its head and took her on a road of discovery, resulting in several other clients' diagnoses, along with her daughters and her own.

After a light bulb moment on a beach in LA, Kim decided it was time to step up and raise awareness of the endless possibilities a neurodiverse brain opens up and change the conversation around ADHD.

Within hours she'd signed up to study with ADDCA (ADD Coaching Academy) and has since developed her ADHD Foundations Masterclasses and group coaching programmes aimed at professionals who want to do business their way and maximise the potential of their neurodiverse brains.

She helps her clients lean into their diversity and overcome procrastination, get on top of overwhelm, master their mindset and increase their confidence so they can be their authentic selves and fly high in life and business.

Kim is the founder of ADHD Brains in Business, a Facebook community for ADHD high flyers (diagnosed or not) to celebrate their ingenious, fast-thinking, sometimes bouncy brains and support each other as they build and lead successful businesses.

https://www.facebook.com/groups/adhdbrainsinbusiness

She coaches clients on a 1-2-1 and group basis and is available to speak at public and corporate events.

Find out more about working with Kim over at

https://kimrainecoaching.com/work-with-me/

Connect with Kim over on her socials at:

facebook.com/KimRaineCoaching
instagram.com/entrepreneursadhdcoach
linkedin.com/in/kimraine

REFERENCES

Chapter 2

ADDCA - Simply ADHD Manual - David Giwerc & Barbara Luther

7 Ways ADHD Can Be Seen in the Brain -

Kailey Spina Horan, Ph.D., LMHC

https://www.psychologytoday.com/us/blog/the-reality-gen-z/202112/7-ways-adhd-can-be-seen-in-the-brain

Chapter 3

The Female Brain - Dr Louann Brizendine

Women With Attention Deficit Disorder Sari Solden MS, LMFT

The Berkeley Girls with ADHD Longitudinal Study

https://chadd.org/wp-content/uploads/2018/10/8C_Wonder-Girls-to-Womder-Women......pdf

References

Dr Lisa Mosconi – TED Talk, How Menopause affects the brain.

https://www.ted.com/talks/
lisa_mosconi_how_menopause_affects_the_brain

Chapter 9

Under-diagnosed and under-treated, girls with ADHD face distinct risks

https://knowablemagazine.org/article/mind/2020/adhd-in-girls-and-women

Knowable Magazine - Women and girls With ADHD

https://youtu.be/aRngPNeLxEM

Chapter 10

Does the perception that stress affects health matter? The association with health and mortality

https://pubmed.ncbi.nlm.nih.gov/22201278/

Chapter 12

Screening of adult ADHD among patients presenting for bariatric surgery

https://pubmed.ncbi.nlm.nih.gov/22161256/

ADHD is a risk factor for overweight and obesity in children

https://www.ncbi.nlm.nih.gov/pmc/articles/PMC3859965/

Chapter 13

Matthew Walker Caffeine -

https://www.youtube.com/watch?v=k5BMGmf1ai0&t=69s

FURTHER READING

The first two are by far the most impactful books I have read on ADHD

Women With Attention Deficit Disorder by Sari Solden MS, LMFT

Scattered Minds by Gabor Mate MD

ADHD 2.0: New Science and Essential Strategies for Thriving with Distraction - from Childhood Through Adulthood by Edward M. Hallowell MD and John J. Ratey MD

Driven to Distraction: Recognizing and Coping with Attention Deficit Disorder

by M D Edward M Hallowell M D and John J Ratey

Faster Than Normal: Turbocharge Your Focus, Productivity, and Success with the Secrets of the ADHD Brain by Peter Shankman, Bernie Wagenblast, et al.

The Body Keeps the Score: Mind, Brain and Body in the Transformation of Trauma

by Sean Pratt, Bessel A. van der Kolk, et al.

*** Why Will No One Play With Me?: The Play Better Plan to Help Kids Make Friends and Thrive by Caroline Maguire.

***I haven't read this book yet, but Caroline was a lecturer at one of my ADDCA sessions, and I was impressed by her knowledge of how ADHD affects children and families. I have since recommended her book and website to clients navigating raising ADHD children who are struggling with friendships and fitting into a neurotypical education system that is buckling at the seams.

Another company and site I recommend to my clients who need support for their children is my good friend Laura Kerbey's site NEST – Neurodivergent Education Support and Training - https://n-est.org/

RECOMMENDED RESOURCES

ADDitude - a website with a wealth of knowledge for all things ADHD https://www.additudemag.com/

ADHD Foundation - https://www.adhdfoundation.org.uk/

ADHD UK - https://adhduk.co.uk/

Information on Access to Work funding -

https://adhduk.co.uk/access-to-work/

ACKNOWLEDGEMENTS

I have spoken for years, no, decades, about writing a book, but it never quite materialised, and now I know why writing a book with ADHD is bloody hard!

None of it would have happened without my right-hand man, my second half and, as corny as it sounds, the wind beneath my wings. I can't believe I have written that, but I cannot think of a better way to convey everything my soul mate, best friend and husband is to me. Thank you for your patience, support, and love, Neil. Along with your never-ending belief in me, however crazy the idea is! *This time next year, Rodney!*

Jordan, my perfect Square Peg who changed my whole world. I am in awe at what a strong, resilient, beautiful woman and mother you have grown into. Keep being you. You are perfect!

Freddie, my kind, charismatic and wise bear. Being your mum keeps me on my toes, your hugs and never-ending smiles fill my heart. You are growing into a fine man, I couldn't be prouder.

And Amaiyah, who has taken my heart to another level. Your sloppy kisses keep me grounded, reminding me to slow down and enjoy what is really important.

My Mum and Dad who always allowed me to be myself and loved my brother and me unconditionally, it's a gift and the start in life many Square Pegs never had. Everything I do is built on the foundations of never-ending support and love you gave us. You did good, and we all love you for it!

A big thank you to Lisa Johnson, Zoë Dew, my travel buddy Mary Ann Smith and all of you who were in that circle in LA, Lucy Rennie, Carol Deveney, Charlie Day, Lauren Prentice, Matt Boyles, Tom Stanhope, Caro Syson, Inge Hunter, Chantelle Davison, Debbie Marks, Yvonne Phillip, Gillian Park, Renee Houtstra, Megan Parker, Emma Morby, Sarah Waldbuesser, Yvonne Bridges, Jenny Drew, Joanne Fisher, Sarah Poynton-Ryan, Nicola Rowley, Niki Matyjasik, Alexandra Metcalfe-Hume and Charlotte Wibberley, (I hope I've mentioned you all).

It wasn't just my business that changed that day. Your support gave me the courage to step up and tell the world I have ADHD. Your ongoing encouragement has got me to this place – thank you!

To Jo & Tina, thank you. Your diagnosis and journey set me on this path. Watching your transformations was an education and an inspiration.

And all my clients who have taught me so much and always pushed me to keep learning and develop so I can be the best coach for you. Especially the BABEs, where I know there were several undiagnosed, unaware struggling Square Pegs. If I haven't put it myself, I hope this book makes it into your hands one day – I wish I knew then what I know now!

To all of the men and women in my ADHD Brains In Business Community and programmes who inspire me to create a better understanding of what ADHD is and the strategies to make it bearable.

To Mia, my niece, for helping me edit, even when the Covid kicked in. You are an angel.

And Suzanne, what can I say? Thank you probably doesn't cover it! God bless your thoroughness!

And finally, to my people, Claire, Carls, Caz, Becs, Char, Kathy, Ant, Spencer, and the Bookham and Oak massive whose company I can always be myself in.